JN101345

社会　Social Studies
subject 4

図工　Arts and Crafts
subject 5

教職英語検定とは

教職英語検定は、日本のグローバル化に対応し、小学校から高校までの学校教育を担う

教職員や教職員を目指す学生が、英語による授業・教科指導を行う力(教職英語と定義)

を習得し、その習得した英語力を知ることを目的としています。

教職英語検定の特色

教職英語検定は、文部科学省の学習指導要領を基本として、日本の公立学校教育の現場に

即した教職英語を習得でき、また習得した力を知ることができることが大きな特色です。

本検定は、小学校教諭用・中学校教諭(理数)・高校教諭(理数)別に、レベルは、基礎、標準、

実践の三つに分けて実施します。

検定は、基礎はリスニングと筆記、標準はリスニングと筆記と英作文、実践はリスニング

と筆記と英作文を一次試験、グループ討議を二次試験とする構成です。

出題の範囲は、小学校教諭用については、基礎、標準レベルは、低学年から高学年までの

算数・国語・理科・社会・図工・体育・音楽・家庭科の科目及び対応する学習指導要領、

実践レベルは、総合学習、児童教育に関する研究。論文が加わります。

中学校教諭用並びに高校教諭用については、基礎、標準レベルは1年生から3年生までの

数学、理科の科目及び対応する学習指導要領、実践レベルは、総合学習、中等教育または

高等教育に関する研究、論文が加わります。

高校教諭用の理科は、物理、化学からの2教科選択です。

本書は、小学校教諭向けのテキスト第2巻で、社会、図工、体育、音楽、家庭科の科目が
収録されています。

算数、国語、理科は、小学校教諭向けのテキスト第1巻に掲載されています。

各教科の内容は、学習指導要領を踏まえて、日本の教育方法に沿っています

本書の特色

01
各教科の単元ごとに分かれており、学年をまたぐ単元については、低学年、中学年、
高学年の順に配置し、取り上げた学年を参考表記しています。

02
全て授業として構成されています。文中に使用している「」、『』は、伝聞あるいは区別・強調
が必要な場合につけており、本来の使用方法とは異なりますが、誤用ではありません。

03
人物の呼称については、英語圏では、Mr. Mrs. Ms. を名前の前につけたり、ファーストネーム
を使うことが多くありますが、日本の生活慣習から違和感を生じないよう、本テキストでは、
児童は「○○ - san」、先生は「○○ sensei」を使用しています。

04
ローマ字は学校教育の指導に則り、原則、訓令式で記載しています。英語での表記ができない
日本語（例えば本は2冊、傘なら2本等の助数詞）は、英語のページであっても、
英語もしくはローマ字をつけて日本語を記載しています。この場合のローマ字は、英語を
母国語とするネイティブスピーカーが、訓令式では発音に支障が生じるため、ヘボン式で
記載しています。

05
各シーンは、左のページに日本語、右のページに英語が記載されています。
記載されている英語は、日本語授業を直訳するのではなく、内容を基本として、
英会話らしい表現で記載しています。

本書が学校教育を担う教職員の皆様の英語力向上の一助になることを願っております。

教材制作部一同

社会 Social Studies

社会
subject 4

Social Studies

地図

地形図と地図記号

中学年

先生

1 地図を見てください。

2 地図のどちらがどの方向かわかりますか。

3 地図は、原則、北が上になっています。

4 これが方位を表す記号です。

5 矢印が付いているのが北です。反対側が南、右が東、左が西です。

6 こちらの地図を見てください。

7 この地図では、高いところは茶色に、少し高いところは緑色に、低いところは黄色に色分けしてあります。

8 土地には、住むのに適した低くて平たんな土地と山や台地といった高い土地があります。

9 土地の高さを標高とか海抜といいます。

10 等高線とは、地図上の土地の高さを表すもので、海面からの高さが同じ所を結んだ線を上から見たものです。

11 等高線の間隔と土地の傾きは、「広い＝緩やか」、「狭い＝急」という公式で暗記するのではなく、断面図で理解することが大切です。

12 また、地図には、地図記号というマークを使います。

13 例えば、この記号をみてください。

14 これは、神社を表す記号です。これは、交番や、警察の記号です。

15 今から、地図記号の一覧表と町探検に使った地図の道路だけ書いてある白地図を配りますから、黒板に張ってある探検地図を見ながら、地図記号を書き込んでください。

探 検 地 図
Exploration Map

Westeland 荒れ地

Cemetery 墓地　Shrine 神社　City hall 市役所　Town hall Village office 町村役場　Hot spring 温泉

Field 地

Rice field 田

Coniferous forest 針葉樹林　High school 高等学校　Post office 郵便局　Hospital 病院　Health center 保健所　Nursing home 老人ホーム

Hardwood forest 広葉樹林　Elementary school Junior high school 小中学校　(大) University 大学　(専) Vocational school 専門学校　(短大) Junior college 短期大学　Plant 工場

Orchard 果樹園　Court 裁判所　Police station 警察署　Police box 交番　Fire station 消防署　Library 図書館

Lighthouse 灯台　Fishing port 漁港　Harbor 港　Museum 博物館・美術館

Map

Topographic maps and map symbols

Grade 3 & 4

Teacher

1 Now, I want you to look at the map.

2 Do you know which direction is where on the map?

3 Well, on a standard map, as a rule the top of the map is north.

4 Here we see the symbol of a compass.

The direction the arrow is pointing is north, and the opposite direction is the south.

5 The right is east, and the left is west.

6 Please look at the map again.

You can see the map is color coordinated, right? The highest elevated areas are in brown,

7 the middle-elevated areas are shown in green, and the lowest land areas are shown in yellow.

There are two types of land: low, flat land suitable for living on and high land such as

8 mountains and plateaus.

9 These lines are called contour lines or just contours. The land's height is expressed in altitude.

10 In other words, the height above the sea level.

The distance between contour lines and the slope of the land should not be memorized with

the formula "wide = gentle" and "narrow = steep". Instead, it is important to understand with

11 a cross-sectional view.

12 We have map symbols for the map.

13 For example, look at this symbol.

14 This is the symbol for a shrine. And this is the symbol for a police box or a police station.

Now, I am now going to give out a list of map symbols and a blank map from our last town

exploration, but only showing the roads. Please draw the symbols on your map while referring

15 to the exploration map on the blackboard.

社会 Social Studies

地図

地球

先生

地球儀には、横線が引いてありますね。それと上と下を結ぶ縦線が引いてあります。

この横線を緯線、縦線を経線といいます。

赤道というのは、春分と秋分の日に、太陽が真上にくる地点を結んだ線です。

経線は、イギリスにあるグリニッジ天文台より東を「東経」、西を「西経」と言い、それぞれ180度まであります。子午線とも言います。

緯線は赤道をゼロ度とし、南北へそれぞれ「南緯」「北緯」と測り、両極で90度にまであります。

子午線と呼ばれるのは、十二支で方向を表したときの子（北）、午（南）の呼び名に由来しています。

地球は、太陽を後転することで、太陽の日光を浴びていますね。

太陽が真上にくる赤道付近はもっとも熱い地域で上下極の端は太陽の光が届きつらいため、氷で覆われています。

赤道付近で、気温が18度の下回らない地域を熱帯といい、温暖で四季がある温帯、北極にむけた冷帯、年間平均気温が10度以下の北極や南極の寒帯があり、それらがさらに細かい気候に分かれています。

日本やアメリカ、ヨーロッパなど多くの経済的に豊かな国の多くは温帯にあります。

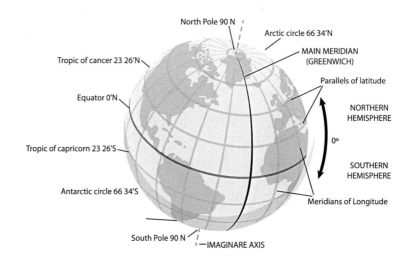

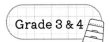

社会

Social Studies

Map
Topographic maps and map symbols

Teacher

1. There is a horizontal line drawn on the globe. And there's a vertical line drawn between the top and the bottom.

2. The horizontal line is called latitude and the vertical line is called longitude.

3. The equator is the line connecting the points where the sun is directly above the equator on the vernal and autumnal equinoxes.

   The longitude that is to the east is called the east longitude and the one to the west is called the west longitude, each are up to 180 degrees from the Greenwich Observatory in England.

4. It is also called the meridian or shigosen.

5. The lines of latitude measure the equator at zero degrees from north to south and north to north, respectively, and extend to 90 degrees at the poles.

6. The name "Shigosen" is derived from the names for the Shi (north) and the Go (south) when directions are represented by the twelve signs of the Chinese zodiac.

7. The earth is bathed in sunlight as it orbits the sun, right?

8. The area near the equator, where the sun is directly above us, is the hottest region, and the upper and lower polar edges are covered with ice because it is hard for the sun's rays to reach them.

   The region near the equator where the temperature does not fall below 18 degrees Celsius is called the tropical zone. There is a temperate zone with warm temperatures and four seasons , a cold zone towards the North Pole, and a cold zone at the North and South poles where the

9. average annual temperature is below 10 degrees Celsius.

10. Many economically rich countries such as Japan, the U.S., and Europe are in the temperate zone.

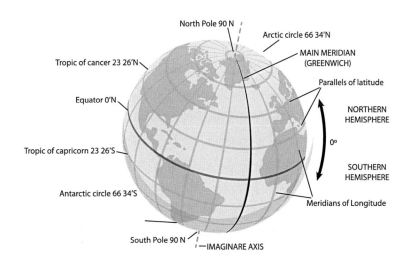

North Pole 90 N

Arctic circle 66 34'N

MAIN MERIDIAN (GREENWICH)

Tropic of cancer 23 26'N

Parallels of latitude

Equator 0'N

NORTHERN HEMISPHERE

0°

Tropic of capricorn 23 26'S

SOUTHERN HEMISPHERE

Antarctic circle 66 34'S

Meridians of Longitude

South Pole 90 N

—IMAGINARE AXIS

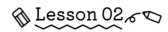
中学年

暮らしを守る

消防・警察

先生

1 来週、消防署の見学に行きます。

2 見学に先立って、消防署の仕事について学習しましょう。

3 消防署は、火事がおきた時に消火する仕事です。

それと救急車があって、119番に電話すると病気の人やけがをした人を病院に連れて

行ってくれます。火事は、家や山などが燃えることです。火災は、火事によって、

4 家が燃えたり、焼け死んだり、やけどを負う災害です。

火事が起きる原因は、たばこの不始末、焚火の消し忘れ、料理の際の過熱等がありますが、

5 さらに放火もあります。

地震が発生すると、調理中の油に火が引火して火事が発生したり、ガス管が折れて

6 噴き出したガスに引火して火事になったりします。

火事は起きないようにみんなで注意しなければなりませんが、もし発生したら早いうちに

消火をすることが大切ですから、火事を発見したらすぐに近くにいる大人の人に伝えるか、

7 携帯や公衆電話から119番に通報します。

先生

1 警察署見学に先立って、警察の仕事を学習しましょう。

2 日本は世界でも安全な国としてトップクラスです。

その理由に、交番や駐在所といった細かな警察網が犯罪予防に

3 つながっていると言われています。

4 私たちの身近なところに警察署があって、交番がありますね。

警察の仕事は、生活の安全を守るということにあります。このために、犯罪が起きないよう

5 にパトロールを行ったり、交通ルールを守っているか監視をしたり、指導をしています。

6 先ほど、日本が世界でも安全な国のトップレベルだといいましたね。

その理由として、交番・派出所など細かな警察網があって犯罪予防につながっていると

7 いいましたが、そのほかにも理由があります。

もっとも重要なのは、私たち日本人のきまりを守ることへの意識の高さと、道徳心の高さ

8 にあります。

9 忘れ物、落し物が届けられて持ち主に戻っているという社会はそうそう世界にありません。

10 拾ったら得をした、自分のものにしてしまうという国が大半です。

11 日本に観光にきた外国人の方が感心するのは特にこのことです。

12 また、交通機関での整列乗車のように、みんなで譲合いをする意識の高さにあります。

13 その上に、銃や刃物の個人所有の規制、警察への信頼の高さが安全を維持しています。

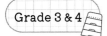
Grade 3 & 4

Living Safely

Fire and Police

Teacher

1. Next week, we are going to take a tour of a fire station.

2. Prior to the visit, let's learn about people's jobs at the fire station.

3. The fire department is responsible for putting out fires.

They also have ambulances that take sick or injured people to the hospital when they call 119.

A fire typically refers to one that happens to a house or forest. In contrast, a fire disaster refers

4. to incidents caused by a fire, such as a total burn down of a house, death, and burn injuries.

Fires can be caused by the careless use of cigarettes, forgetting to extinguish bonfires,

5. and overheating during cooking. Also, it could be due to arson.

When an earthquake strikes, cooking oil could catch a fire, or even a gas pipe could break and

6. then catch fire.

Everyone must take precautions to prevent fires from starting, but if a fire does start, it is

important to extinguish it as soon as possible, so immediately tell an adult nearby or call 119

7. from a cell phone or public phone.

Teacher

1. let's learn more about the responsibilities of the police.

2. Japan is one of the safest countries in the world.

The police boxes spread across the country are considered one of

3. the primary factors that help to prevent crime.

4. In Japan, there are police stations and police boxes, right?

The police's main purpose is to keep us safe in daily life. For this, they continually patrol the

5. city to prevent crimes, as well as monitor and provide guidance towards the safety of the city.

6. Earlier, I said that Japan is one of the safest countries in the world.

I mentioned that one of the reasons for this is because there is a detailed network of police

7. stations that are spread across the city. But, there's also another reason.

The most important reason is actually our high consciousness on following the rules, as well as

8. our high sense of morals.

9. There are very few places in the world where lost belongings eventually get back to their owners.

In most countries, many people think that they are lucky when they find a lost item, and they

10. keep it for themselves.

11. This is a part of our culture that foreign visitors are especially impressed with.

Equally, our consideration for others in public transportation, such as lining up properly when

12. riding trains, is highly regarded.

On top of that, there are tight restrictions for possessing guns and knives, as well as a high

13. trust that people have towards the police.

すみよいくらしをつくる

中学年

先生 📣

昔は水道もなく、井戸を掘って、その井戸水を飲んだり、水洗トイレがなくて、排泄物は溜めてから捨てたり、肥料として畑に撒いていた時代が何百年も続いていたことを学習しました。

暮らしはどんどんとよくなっていますが、この暮らしがどうやって支えられているかを学習します。水をためる施設を昔はため池といい、1300年前にはすでに日本でも作られていました。

もともとため池と言っていましたが、技術的に川をせき止める堤防の高さを高くできるようになり、15m以上の高さの堤防がある場合、ダムと呼ぶようになりました。

ため池やダムの設置により、安定して水は供給されます。

しかし、川の水にはいろいろなものが混じっていて、

そのままで飲むことは体に危険なこともあります。

そのため、いくつかの施設を通して、きれいな水にしています。

ところで、上水道が整備されて、日本ではそのまま蛇口から飲めるほど

きれいな水が供給できていますが、世界には飲み水が足りない国がたくさんあります。

それは、地球上の水のほとんどが海水で、川や湖、地下水など飲み水として使える水が、わずか0.008%だからです。

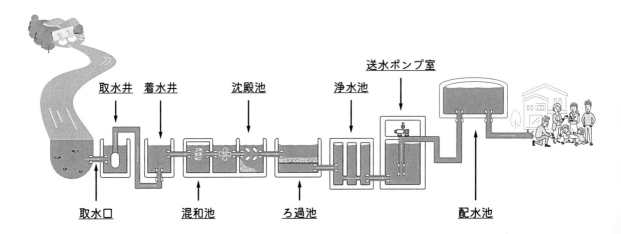

送水ポンプ室

取水井　着水井　　　沈殿池　　　　　浄水池

取水口　　　混和池　　　ろ過池　　　　　　配水池

Grade 3 & 4

Creating Comfortable Lives

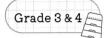

Teacher
📢

When we studied about ancient lifestyles before, we learned that there was no convenient working water system like now, so people would dig a well to get drinking water. There were no flush toilets so people had to gather a certain level of excrement before disposing of it, or even use it as fertilizer in their gardens. This lifestyle continued for hundreds of years.

Our lifestyles have improved greatly, so let's discuss topics related to our current lifestyle.

In olden times, we called facilities to supply water, ponds, the first of which was built 1,300 years ago in Japan.

But technology has developed and people have become able to build higher walls to stop the flow of rivers. Currently, facilities with walls over 15 meters high are called dams.

Because of these ponds and dams, water can be distributed consistently.

However, there are many different substances found in river water, so it could be dangerous for our health to drink it directly.

We use some special facilities to make the water clean.

In Japan, the water system is organized so that you can drink clean water directly from the tap.

However, there are many countries in the world which have a shortage of clean water.

This is because most of the earth is covered in seawater, which is undrinkable, and freshwater from rivers, lakes, and wells is only 0.008% of all water in the world.

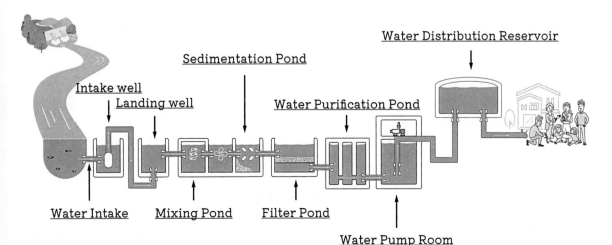

Water Distribution Reservoir

Sedimentation Pond

Intake well
Landing well

Water Purification Pond

Water Intake   Mixing Pond   Filter Pond

Water Pump Room

中学年

すみよいくらしをつくる

先生

1. 上水道のことは理解できました。
2. 川の水をきれいにして、私たちは使っていますね。
3. では、使った水はどうしていますか。
4. 汚いまま流してしまったら、どうなりますか。
5. 汚れた水を直接流すことがないように水道管と同じように下水管という管を通じて、汚れた水を集め、先ほどの川の水を浄水するようにして、きれいな水にして川に流せる仕組みを作っています。
6. これを行っているが下水浄化センターです。

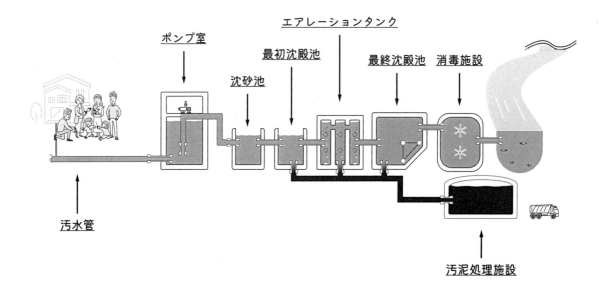

ポンプ室　　　エアレーションタンク

最初沈殿池　　　　最終沈殿池　消毒施設

沈砂池

汚水管

汚泥処理施設

水質検査
Water quality inspection

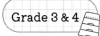
Grade 3 & 4

Creating Comfortable Lives

Teacher

1 | We will now learn about the waterworks.

2 | We use water from the river and purify it, right?

3 | Now, how do we get rid of the waste water we've used?

4 | What would happen if we let the dirty water go into the river?

| Sewer pipes were built to prevent these things from happening. They collect the dirty water

5 | to be purified, and afterwards, release it into a river.

6 | This is called a sewage purification system.

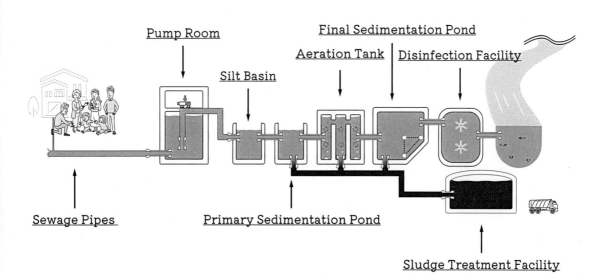

Pump Room

Final Sedimentation Pond

Aeration Tank

Disinfection Facility

Silt Basin

Sewage Pipes

Primary Sedimentation Pond

Sludge Treatment Facility

水質検査
Water quality inspection

日本の気候

先生

1 日本の場合、島国であること、南北に長い国土であること、山林が多いことなどから、気候が地域によって異なっています。

2 日本の気候の特色を見てみましょう。

3 まず、日本の気候の特色というと何が思い浮かびますか。

4 梅雨と台風が一番の特色です。

5 これは、東側に太平洋、西側にユーラシア大陸という条件が、季節によって風向きが変わる季節風の影響により発生します。

6 上空には、冷たく湿ったオホーツク海気団と暖かく湿った小笠原気団があり、気団がぶつかるところを前線といい、雨が降ります。

7 6月頃は、その気団の勢力が拮抗し、前線が動かなくなったり動きがゆっくりになったりするため、長雨になります。

8 6月の長雨を梅雨と書くのは同じ漢字の国として中国も同じですが、日本で梅雨をつゆと読むのは、この時期が梅が完熟してつぶれるほどになる「潰ゆ（つゆ）から来たそうです。

9 台風は、一年中暑い熱帯地方である北緯5度から20度くらいの海上で多く発生しています。

10 このあたりの海は他の場所と比べて海水の温度も高く雲が多いので、台風が渦を巻く力があるためです。

11 台風の進路は、主に上空の風の流れで、概ね決まっています。

12 赤道の近くでは「貿易風」という強い風に流されて西へ進み、日本に近づくと、今度は「偏西風」と呼ぶ強い西風に流されて東へ進みます。

13 日本列島が太平洋高気圧に覆われている7月と8月は、台風が近づけず、北上しますが、9月になると、太平洋高気圧の勢力が弱まり、日本付近に接近、上陸するようになります。

14 そして、10月以降は、北からの高気圧が張り出してくるため、日本より南を通るようになります。

偏西風　7月　8月　9月　6月　10月　11月

10月　6月　11月　12月　貿易風

Climate of Japan

Grade 5 & 6

Teacher

In the case of Japan, the climate differs from region to region due to the fact that Japan is an island nation, has a long land length from north to south, and has many mountainous forests.

Let us take a look at the characteristics of Japan's climate.

What do you think of when you hear the phrase Japanese climate?

The rainy season and typhoons are the most distinctive features.

These are caused by the monsoon winds, which change their direction depending on the season, with the Pacific Ocean to the east and the Eurasian continent to the west.

In the sky, there is the cold and moist Okhotsk high air mass and the warm and moist Ogasawara air mass; the place where these air masses collide is called a front and this collision causes rain.

Around June, these air masses compete with each other and the fronts stop moving or move slowly, resulting in a long rainy season.

In Japan, the word tsuyu (rainy season) comes from the Japanese word tsuyu (ripen), which means "crushed plum" in Japanese, when the plum trees are fully ripened to the point of being crushed.

Typhoons occur mostly in the oceans between 5 and 20 degrees north latitude, which is a tropical region that is hot all year round.

This is because the seas around here have higher sea water temperatures and more clouds than other places, so typhoons have more power to swirl.

The path of a typhoon is generally determined mainly by the wind currents.

Near the equator, typhoons are driven westward by strong trade winds, and as they approach Japan, they are driven eastward by strong westerly winds, which are called westerlies.

In July and August, when the Japanese islands are covered by the Pacific High, typhoons cannot approach Japan and move a northward, but in September, the Pacific High becomes less powerful and approaches and lands near Japan.

Then, from October onward, high pressure from the north will extend out, high pressure from the north will move south of Japan.

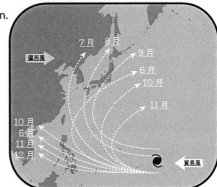

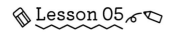
高学年

日本の農業

先生

1 私たちの主食はお米ですね。

2 日本人がお米を主食として食べるようになったのは、縄文時代といって 3,000 年ほど前からです。

3 中国から九州に稲作技術が伝わり、2500 年前にはすでに青森県まで広がっていました。

4 お米が普及したのは、日本の気候が挙げられます。

5 雨が多く降る季節（梅雨）と雨が少なく暑い季節（夏)がある日本の気候がお米づくりに適していたのです。

6 これはタイやインドネシアなどの東南アジアおよび中国などお米の生産量の多い地域に共通するポイントです。

7 少し、お米のことを学習していきましょう。

8 4 月に苗づくりをし、5 月に田起こしと言ってトラクターで土を掘り起こして田植えの準備をし、6 月に水を張って、苗を植えて、9 月に稲刈りをして、籾取りをします。

9 コメ作りは、全国で行われていますが、東北と北陸をあわせて、日本国内の米の生産量の 40% ちかくを生産して「日本の米倉」と呼ばれています。

10 この地方が多いのは、広い平野や盆地があり、さらに雪どけ水などで、川に多くの水があること、品種改良が進み、気温が低くても生産可能になったからです。

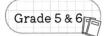
Agriculture in Japan

Teacher

As you may already know, our staple food is rice.

Japanese people began to eat rice as a staple food about 3,000 years ago, during the Jomon Period.

Rice cultivation technology was introduced from China to Kyushu and by 2500 years ago had already spread to Aomori Prefecture.

The climate of Japan is cited as the reason for the spread of rice.

Japan's climate, with its rainy season and hot weather (summer) with little rainfall, was suitable for rice cultivation.

This is a point shared by other Southeast Asian countries, such as Thailand and Indonesia, as well as China and other regions that produce large amounts of rice.

Let's learn a little about rice.

In April, seedlings are grown, in May, a tractor is used to dig up the soil in preparation for rice planting, in June, water is applied, seedlings are planted, and in September, rice is harvested and unhauled.

Rice production is carried out throughout Japan, and the Tohoku and Hokuriku regions together produce nearly 40% of all rice in Japan, earning them the nickname "Japan's Rice Warehouse".

The reason for the large amount of rice produced in this region is the wide plains and basins, the abundance of water in rivers due to snow melt and other factors, and advances in breeding that have made it possible to produce rice even in cooler temperatures.

高学年

日本の農業

先生

1 農業はお米作りだけではありません。

野菜つくりをしている農家を野菜農家、果物を作る場所を果樹園農家といい、肉や牛乳、
2 卵を供給している農家を畜産農家といいます。

野菜、ことにホウレンソウやキャベツ等の葉物は、もぎってから数日しか持ちませんから、
3 できるだけ、大都会の消費地に近いところで生産しています。
4 このような農業を近郊農業といいます。
5 それとは別に、いつスーパーに行っても、キャベツもピーマンもトマトも売っていますね。
6 ミカンのような果物なら、冷凍して販売することが可能ですが、野菜は冷凍に向きません。

そこで、日本が南北に長い国土で、且つ山が多いという地の利を生かして、時期をずらして
7 野菜作りをしています。

例えば、宮崎県や高知県では、冬でも暖かい気候を利用してピーマンなどの促成栽培を、
長野県や群馬県では夏でも涼しい気候を利用して、白菜や等をキャベツなどの抑制栽培を
8 行っています。

先生

1 遺伝子組み換え技術というのを知っていますか。

人に限らず、生き物はすべて細胞からできていて、細胞の中にDNAという物質があり、
2 その中に遺伝子があります。

この遺伝子が、親から子に受け継がれていき、アサガオの種からはアサガオが、
3 スズメのひなはスズメになります。
5 その遺伝子を人間が勝手に他の生き物の遺伝子と組み替えてしまう技術です。

6 これによって、農薬に強い植物や新しい生き物が生まれたりします。

この技術が本当にいいのか、遺伝子を勝手に人間が変えることがよいのかは
7 はっきりしていません。

Agriculture in Japan

Grade 5 & 6

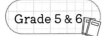

Teacher 📢

1 Agriculture is not only faming.

The farmers who grow vegetables are called vegetable farmers, and those who grow fruits are

2 called orchard farmers.

Vegetables, especially leafy vegetables such as spinach and cabbage, last only a few days after

3 being picked, so they are produced as close to the consumption centers in large cities as possible.

4 This type of agriculture is called suburban agriculture.

5 Whenever I go to the supermarket, cabbages, peppers, and tomatoes are always on sale.

Fruits such as mandarin oranges can be frozen and sold, but vegetables are not suitable

6 for freezing.

Therefore, we take advantage of the fact that Japan is a long country stretching from

7 north to south and is mountainous, and we grow vegetables at different times of the year.

For example, Miyazaki and Kochi prefectures take advantage of their warm winters to

promote the cultivation of green peppers and other vegetables, while Nagano and

Gunma prefectures take advantage of their cool summers to cultivate Chinese cabbage,

8 cabbage, and other vegetables in a controlled manner.

Teacher 📢

1 Do you know what genetic modification technology is?

Not only humans, but all living things are made up of cells, and within each cell is a substance

2 called DNA, which contains genes.

These genes are passed down from parent to child, and a morning glory seed becomes

3 a morning glory, and a sparrow's chick becomes a sparrow.

5 This is a technology in which humans take the liberty of recombining these genes with those

of other living creatures.

6 This can lead to the creation of pesticide-resistant plants and new creatures.

It is not clear whether this technology is really good or not, or whether it is good for humans

7 to change?

日本の水産業

漁業と海

高学年

先生

1 今日は、漁業を中心とする水産業を学習します。

2 漁業と水産業の違いを説明すると、魚を獲るのが漁業、魚を加工したり、魚を獲るだけなく、育てたりするものを含めて水産業といいます。

3 さて、魚はとても健康にいいとTVでもたくさん取り上げています。

4 青魚に含まれるDHAという物質です。

5 DHAというのは、中性脂肪やコルステロール値を下げたり、動脈硬化を予防する効果があります。だから、生活習慣病になりかかっているおじさんやおばさんには大変重要です。

6 DHAは、大変効果のある栄養素ですが、体内で作ることが出来ず、食事でしか摂取できず、不足すると視力が衰えることもわかっています。そして、このDHAを豊富に含んでいるのが青魚です。DHAの効果が科学的に発見されたのは最近です。

7 発見される随分前から、島国で海に囲まれていますから、漁業が盛んでした。

8 それは、日本の回りの海には、暖流・寒流のぶつかる潮目があることや魚のえさになるプランクトンが豊富な大陸棚というゆるやかな傾斜のある海底があり、世界有数の漁場となっているからです。1日1人あたりの魚介類消費量は、168gと世界トップで2位のスペインより1.3倍もあります。

9 漁業や水産業の学習では、まず、この線が引かれていない海の境目について知っておく必要があります。

10 現在のところ、世界の海は、国際法上大きく4つ（領海、接続海域、排他的経済水域、公海）に分けられています。

11 「領海」とは、基線からその外側12海里（約22km）以内の海域で、主権が及びます。

12 「接続海域」とは、基線からその外側24海里（約44km）以内の海域で、さまざまな規制をすることができます。

13 「排他的経済水域」とは、基線からその外側200海里以内の海域（領海を除く）で利用方法について優先権を持っています。

14 「公海」とは各国が自由に自国の旗を掲げて航行できる海域です。

15 日本の国土は約38万㎢で世界第60位ですが、領海と排他的経済水域（EEZ）を合わせると約447万㎢で世界第6位となります。

16 領海では、漁業だけでなく、海底にある様々な資源の掘削権もあり、とても重要です。

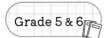 **Lesson 06**

Grade 5 & 6

Japan's Fisheries

Fisheries & Sea

Teacher

Today, we will study the fisheries industry.

First, let's explain the difference between fishing and the fisheries industry. Fishing is simply the catching of fish, while the fisheries industry includes processing and raising fish as well as catching fish.

Now, fish is very healthy and has been featured a lot on TV.

It is because of a substance called DHA, which is found in blue fish.

DHA is effective in lowering neutral fat and cholesterol levels and preventing arteriosclerosis.

So it is very important for older man or women who are suffering from lifestyle-related illnesses.

DHA is a very effective nutrient, but it cannot be produced by the body and can only be consumed through food. Blue fish is a rich source of DHA. The benefits of DHA were only recently discovered scientifically.

Long before it was discovered, Japan was an island nation surrounded by oceans and had a thriving fishing industry.

Japan is one of the world's leading fishing grounds because of the tidal flanks where warm and cold currents collide and the gently sloping continental shelf, which is rich in plankton, which is a food source for fish. The amount of seafood consumed per person per day is 168 grams in Japan, 1.3 times as much as Spain, ranked number two.

In learning about fisheries and the fishing industry, it is first necessary to know about the boundaries of the oceans where these lines are obviously not physically drawn.

Currently, the world's oceans are divided into four major categories under international law (territorial sea, connected waters, exclusive economic zones, and international waters).

The "territorial sea" is the sea area within 12 nautical miles (approximately 22 km) outside the baseline, and is subject to sovereignty.

The "connected waters " is the sea area within 24 nautical miles (about 44 km) outside the baseline, where a nation can impose various regulations.

The "exclusive economic zone" is the area within 200 nautical miles (excluding other country's territorial sea), and a country has priority over others in terms of usage.

The " International waters " are areas in which countries can freely navigate under their own flags.

Japan is the 60th largest country in the world in terms of land area (approximately 380,000 km^2), but when territorial waters and exclusive economic zones (EEZs) are combined, Japan ranks 6th in the world in terms of land area (approximately 4.47 million km^2).

The territorial waters are very important not only for fishing, but also for the right to drill for various resources on the seabed.

日本の水産業

漁業の種類

高学年

先生

漁業は、漁獲するまでの距離によって、3つに分けられています。

「遠洋漁業」:複数の船で船団を組み、数十日～数ヶ月世界の海で漁をする漁業です。
戦後急速に増えていったが船の燃料費の高騰、200海里規制により、漁場は狭くなり
急速に衰えています。

「沖合漁業」:ほぼ日帰り可能な海域で、動力が10t以上の漁船を使った漁業でしたが、2
00海里規制で、漁獲高が次第に減少しています。

「沿岸漁業」:ほぼその国の領海内で行なわれる漁法です。
漁獲量はほぼ横ばいですが、近年では、家庭や工場からの排水で海が汚れ、
魚が少なくなっています。

遠洋漁業や沖合漁業が急速に衰える中で、消費に見合う漁獲のための工夫がなされていて、
それが、育てる漁業です。

育てる漁業は主に養殖業と栽培漁業の2つがあり、まだい、ほたて貝、かきなどの
中高級魚を育てています。

養殖業と栽培漁業の大きな違いは、稚魚を海や川に放流するかどうかです。

養殖業では、養殖場で卵をかえしたり稚魚を海から取ってきたりして、いけすで育てて、
いけすから水揚げします。

栽培漁業では、栽培虚業センターで卵をかえして、稚魚をいけすなどで育てたうえで川や
海に放流し、自然の中で漁獲します。

養殖業・栽培漁業は生産を計画的に行い、収入が安定しています、プランクトンの増加に
より海面が赤褐色になるという赤潮という現象で、被害にあうこともあります。

赤潮がおきると、プランクトンが大発生し、水中の酸素が欠乏して、魚が水中で呼吸でき
ない事態になってしまいます。

また、育てる漁業というより、餌付け漁業といえる海洋牧場も作られています。

海洋牧場とは、海中に人工的に魚の住処を作り、
音の合図でえさ場に集まる工夫をして、魚を育てます。

Grade 5 & 6

Japan's Fisheries

Fisheries & Sea

Teacher

Fisheries are divided into three categories based on the distance between the shore and the area to be fished.

Open sea fishing is those in which multiple vessels form a fleet and fish in the world's oceans for over ten days to several months. The number of vessels has increased rapidly since the end of World War II, but the fishing grounds have become narrower due to soaring fuel costs for vessels and the 200-nautical-mile limit, and the industry is rapidly declining.

Offshore fishing: Fishing with vessels of 10 tons or more in areas where it is possible to make a day trip, but catches are gradually declining due to the 200-nautical mile limit.

Coastal fishing: Fishing is conducted almost entirely within a country's territorial waters.

The catch has remained mostly unchanged, but in recent years, wastewater from homes and factories has polluted the ocean, resulting in fewer fish.

While pelagic and offshore fisheries are rapidly declining, fishermen are devising new ways to catch fish for consumption, and one of this is by raising fish in fisheries.

There are two main types of fisheries: aquaculture and cultivated fisheries, which grows medium- to high-end fish such as mud snails, scallops, and oysters.

The main difference between aquaculture and cultivated fisheries is whether or not the fry is released into the sea or rivers.

In aquaculture, the eggs are reared at the farm and the fry are taken from the sea, raised in fish ponds, and then unloaded from the ponds. In aquaculture, after harvesting eggs or fry from either the wild or raised fish, the young fish are raised in captivity, and then sold for consumption.

In the cultivated fisheries industry, after hatching eggs and raising the fry in a cultivation fishing center, the young fish are released into the oceans and rivers to be caught in the wild.

Aquaculture and cultivated fisheries are planned, and their income is stable, but they are sometimes affected by the red tide, a phenomenon in which the sea surface turns reddish brown due to an increase in plankton.

When a red tide occurs, plankton blooms and the oxygen in the water is depleted, making it impossible for fish to breathe underwater.

Marine ranches are also being created, which are more like feeding fisheries than nurturing fisheries.

In marine ranching, fish are artificially created to live in the sea, and are attracted to the feeding grounds by sound cues.

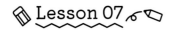
高学年

日本の工業

先生
📢

1 今日からは工業について学習します。

工業とは、農業や水産業、鉱業などの自然に存在する資源や生産物に、道具 や機械で

なんらかの加工を施して、様々な製品を一定の場所（たとえば工場）で一定量、連続的に

2 製造する産業をいいます。

簡単な道具や機械を使って行う工業はかなり古くから行われていましたが、江戸時代まで

3 は手工業の域を越えませんでした。

4 明治時代になると欧米から近代工業を学びます。

5 大規模な製鉄工場や製糸工場を作ります。これが日本の工業化の始まりとなります。

6 日本の工業の特色は、まず、自動車工業を始めとする機械工業が盛んなことにあります。

7 自動車工業は世界第3位の生産台数です。

8 次に、中小工場の多さです。

日本には 40 万の工場があり、そのうちの 99% 以上の工場が、働く人 300 人以下の

9 中小企業です。

10 工業が発達するためには、広い工業用地と豊かな工業用水が必要です。

また、原料や製品の輸送に便利であることが必要で、大量に重い物を輸送できる船舶が

11 利用できる海岸沿いが適しています。

このような立地条件がそろった関東から九州の海岸沿いに、多数の工場があり、工業地帯

12 を構成していて、これを太平洋ベルト地帯と呼んでいます。

一方で、焼き物（陶磁器）や塗り物（漆器）、和紙等伝統工芸を受け継いで製品を作る

13 伝統工業も多くあります。

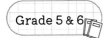
Japan's Industries

Grade 5 & 6

Teacher

1 | Today, we will start learning about industry.

Industry refers to industries that continuously manufacture various products in at Industry refers to one that continuously manufactures various products in fixed quantities at fixed locations (e.g., factories) by processing naturally occurring resources and products with tools

2 | and machines, such as agriculture, fisheries, and mining.

Industries using simple tools and machines have been in place for quite some time, but did not

3 | go beyond the realm of handicrafts until the Edo period (1603-1867).

In the Meiji Era (1868-1912), the country learned about modern industry from Europe and

4 | the United States.

5 | Large-scale iron and silk mills were built. This marked the beginning of Japan's industrialization.

Japan's industry is characterized, first of all, by its thriving machinery industry, including

6 | the automobile industry.

7 | The automobile industry is the world's third largest producer.

8 | Second, there are many small and medium-sized factories.

There are 400,000 factories in Japan, and more than 99% of them are small and medium-sized

7 | enterprises (SMEs) employing less than 300 workers.

10 | Industrial development requires large industrial sites and abundant industrial water.

In addition, the transportation of raw materials and products must be convenient, and coastal

11 | areas with access to vessels that can transport large volumes of heavy materials are ideal.

The Pacific Belt Zone is an industrial zone with many factories located along the coast from

12 | Kanto to Kyushu where these conditions are met.

On the other hand, there are also many traditional industries that produce products based on

13 | traditional crafts such as pottery, lacquerware, and Japanese paper.

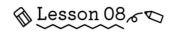
国ということ、国家ということ

先生 📢

1 私たちは日本国という国に住んでいます。世界にはたくさんの国があることは学習しました。

では、この国って何でしょうか。少なくとも、一定の地域で一定の人数が共同体を形成し、

共同体を維持するための納税制度をもち、他からの侵略を防ぐ手段を講じる体制がある

2 のが国家です。

3 なお、国家は、他の国家から、独立した国であると認められることが必要です。

一国家は一つの組織として動くため、意思の決定と実行が必要となりますから、指導者が

4 必要になります。指導者になると大きな権限を持ちます。

権力が集中して横暴な政治が行わることを防ごうとして、権力の性質に応じて区別し、

それぞれ異なる機関に分離し、相互に抑制と均衡を保たせ緊張状態を維持させようという

5 発想が生まれました。

これが三権分立という考えで、1700年代のモンテスキューというフランスの哲学者が

6 唱えました。

7 ポイントは権力の「区別」「分離」「抑制と均衡」です。

8 三権分立の「三権」とは、立法・行政・司法です。

日本は、第2次世界大戦での敗戦を機に、国の最高のきまりである憲法で、それまでの

国の主体を天皇という考えから国民という考えに変え、天皇は日本の象徴であるとし、

国民の様々な権利を明記し、戦争を放棄すると定めるとともに、それまで天皇に集中

9 していた立法・行政・司法の三権を分立とする内容に変更しました。

10 1つ目の立法とは「法律を作る」機能です。

11 日本であれば、国会が唯一の国としての立法機関にあたります。

2つ目の行政とは、「国として、国民に対してのサービス」を行う機能です。

行政府とは、国民が税金で国家公務員や地方公務員を雇って国民の為に仕事をする所です。

12 その行政府のトップである各省庁の大臣を決めるのが内閣総理大臣です。

13 3つ目の司法とは、「ルールに基づいて裁く」機能です。裁判所ですね。

特に司法権は重要です。それは、司法権に「人権の保障・救済」の機能が求められている

からです。立法権の作った悪法に基づいて不条理に逮捕されてしまった人たちを裁判で

14 救済できます。行政権が法を濫用して侵そうとする人権を裁判でしっかり保障できます。

特に民主国家では立法権・行政権ともに政党政治の影響を受けやすいという面があります。

15 司法権は独立性があれば、どこからも干渉されず、公正な裁きを行うことができます。

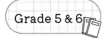

Grade 5 & 6

Nations and States

Teacher

We live in a country called Japan. We have learned that there are many countries in the world. Then, what is a country? At least a nation has a system in which a certain number of people form a community in a certain area, a tax payment system to maintain the community, and measures to prevent invasion from other countries.

A state must be recognized by other states as an independent state.

Because a nation operates as a single entity, it needs to make and carry out decisions, and therefore it needs a leader. When you become a leader, you have great authority. In order to prevent the concentration of power and tyrannical politics, the idea of separating power according to its nature, separating it into different institutions, and maintaining a state of tension by maintaining checks and balances was born.

This is the idea of separation of powers, which was advocated by a French philosopher named Montesquieu in the 1700s.

The key points are "distinction," "separation," and "checks and balances of power".

The "three powers" of the separation of powers are the legislative, executive, and judicial. After Japan's defeat in World War II, Japan adopted the Constitution, the supreme rule of the nation, to change the concept of the nation from the Emperor to that of the people, and established the Emperor as the symbol of Japan. In addition to stipulating the various rights of the people and renouncing war, it was also changed to divided the three powers of legislature, administration, and judiciary, which had been concentrated in the hands of the Emperor until then.

The first, legislation, is the function of making laws.

In Japan, the Diet is the sole national legislative body.

The second is the executive, which performs the function of providing services to the people as the state. The executive branch is the place where the citizens employ national and local government officials with their tax money to do work for the people. The Prime Minister is the head of the executive branch and decides the ministers of each ministry and agency.

The third, the judiciary, is the function of judging based on rules. It is a court of law. Judicial power is particularly important. This is because the judicial power is required to have the function to guarantee and remedy human rights. Courts can help those who have been unjustly arrested based on bad laws created by the legislative power.

The courts can firmly guarantee human rights that the executive power tries to violate by abusing the law. Especially in a democratic state, both legislative and executive powers are susceptible to party politics. If the judicial power is independent, it can adjudicate fairly without interference from any source.

高学年

三権分立

立法・行政・司法

先生

1. 立法府である国会を学習します。

2. 日本の国会は、衆議院と参議院の二院制です。

3. これはより慎重な審議を行うためです。

4. 国会議員は選挙によって選ばれます。

国会は、法律を制定するという役割以外に予算を決める、行政部の長となる内閣総理大臣を決める、他国との条約を承認する、三権の一つである司法を担う裁判官を裁判する弾劾裁判所を設置するなどの役割を担っています。

5. また、憲法を改正する発議権を持っています。

6. 二院制ですが、衆議院に優越権がある役割があります。

7. 参議院議員は任期6年です。

衆議院議員は任期4年ですが、優越権のある役割がある引換えに任期途中でも内閣により解散される場合があります。

8.

先生

1. 行政府である内閣を学習しましょう。

2. 内閣総理大臣は国会議員の中から指名されます。

内閣は、国の予算を国会に提出する、外国との条約を締結する、政令を策定する、最高裁判所の長官を指名し、他の裁判官を指名する、天皇の国事行為に助言と承認を与えるなどの役割を担っています。

3.

4. 内閣は、1名の内閣総理大臣と、14名〜17名の国務大臣からなる組織です。

5. 内閣総理大臣は首相とも呼ばれます。

7. 内閣総理大臣は、そのときの国会議員でなければならず、国会により指名されます。

国務大臣とは、厚生労働省の大臣、文部科学省の大臣や農林水産省の大臣など、つまり省の大臣のことです。

8.

7. 国務大臣の過半数は、国会議員でなければなりません。

Grade 5 & 6

The Separation of Powers

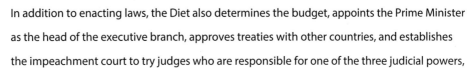

Judicature · Legislative · Executive

Teacher

1. This lesson focuses on the Diet, the legislative branch of government.

Japan has a bicameral legislature, consisting of the House of Representatives and

2. the House of Councilors.

3. This is to allow for more careful deliberations.

4. Members of the Diet are elected through elections.

In addition to enacting laws, the Diet also determines the budget, appoints the Prime Minister

as the head of the executive branch, approves treaties with other countries, and establishes

the impeachment court to try judges who are responsible for one of the three judicial powers,

5. the judiciary.

It also has the power to propose amendments to the Constitution.

6. Although the House of Councilors is bicameral, the House of Representatives has a dominant role.

7. Members of the House of Councilors serve six-year terms.

Members of the House of Representatives serve a four-year term, but may be dissolved by

8. the Cabinet even during their term in exchange for a superior role.

Teacher

1. Let us learn about the Cabinet, the executive branch of government.

2. The Prime Minister is appointed from among the members of the Diet.

The Cabinet is responsible for submitting the national budget to the Diet, concluding treaties

with foreign countries, formulating cabinet orders, nominating the Chief Justice of the Supreme

3. Court and other judges, and giving advice and approval to the emperor's acts of state.

4. The Cabinet is an organization consisting of one Prime Minister and 14 to 17 Ministers of State.

5. The Prime Minister is also called the Head of State.

7. The Prime Minister must be a member of the Diet at the time and is appointed by the Diet.

Ministers of State are ministers of ministries, such as the Minister of Health, Labor and Welfare,

the Minister of Education, Culture, Sports, Science and Technology, and

8. the Minister of Agriculture, Forestry and Fisheries.

9. The majority of the Ministers of State must be members of the Diet.

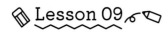

三権分立

立法・行政・司法

高学年

先生

1. 司法である裁判所を学習しましょう

　裁判とは、国民どうしの争いごとを解決したり、犯罪を疑われている人の罪のあるなしを

2. 決めることです。

3. 司法権は、裁判所しか持つことが出来ませんので、国会も内閣も、裁判には口出しできません。

4. 裁判所には、最高裁判所と下級裁判所があります。

　裁判の結果に不服のときは、さらに上級の裁判所に、同じ事件について、訴えることが

5. 合計で3回まででき、裁判の三審制といいます。

　そして、どんな事件でも、最高裁判所が最後の裁判所で最高裁判所の判決に

6. したがわなければなりません。

7. 裁判員制度が、2009年（平成21年）から始まりました。

　裁判員制度は、殺人事件などの刑事事件についての裁判で、国民の中からくじで

8. 選ばれた人が裁判員になって、罪のあるなしを裁判官とともに決める制度です。

9. この制度の考えは、国民のさまざまな考えを裁判にも活用しようという制度です。

　この裁判員制度は、地方裁判所で行われる刑事事件のうち、殺人事件や放火事件などの

10. 罪の重い事件の裁判で、行われることになっています。

```
            最高裁判所
         ↑           ↑
            高等裁判所
      ↑      ↑       ↑
   地方裁判所      家庭裁判所
      ↑
   簡易裁判所
```

Grade 5 & 6

The Separation of Powers

Judicature · Legislative · Executive

Teacher

1. Let's learn about the court, the judiciary.

A trial is to settle disputes among citizens and to decide whether a person suspected of

2. a crime is guilty or not.

3. Since only the courts have judicial power, neither the Diet nor the Cabinet can interfere with trials.

4. There are two types of courts: the Supreme Court and lower courts.

If a person is dissatisfied with the outcome of a trial, he/she can appeal to a higher court up to

5. three times for the same case, which is called the three-trial system.

In any case, the Supreme Court is the final court and must decide the case according to

6. the decision of the Supreme Court.

7. The jury system began in 2009.

The jury system is a system in which people selected by lottery from among the public serve

as judges in criminal trials, such as murder cases, and decide with the judge whether or

8. not a person is guilty of a crime.

9. The idea of this system is to utilize various ideas of the public in the trials.

This jury system is to be used in the trials of serious criminal cases, such as murder and arson

10. cases, which are held in district courts.

```
                    Supreme Court
                  ↑              ↑
                    High Court
              ↑          ↑         ↑
      District Court           Family Court
              ↑
            Summary Court
```

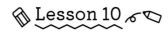

地方自治

高学年

先生

今日は、地方自治を学習します。私たちは日本という国の東京都に住んでいます。

日本では、日本を 47 の都道府県に区分して、各県にこれまでの歴史的なつながりと住んでいる住民の数を考えて市町村という小区分をするというルールを作りました。

この区分に従って活動する職業を公務員といい、住民の考えや意見を反映させていく代表を議員や首長と呼び、住民の選挙で選ぶことで、地域の多数意見が反映される制度としています。

議員や首長も警察官や市役所の職員と同様に公務員です。

この、それぞれの地域に住む住民がその地域の政治を自主的に行うことを地方自治といい、その地方自治を行う単位を地方公共団体または地方自治体といいます。

市の基準は地方自治法という法律に決まっていて、町の基準は都道府県が独自に決めることが出来、市も町にも該当しない地域が村という地方公共団体になります。

市は 5 万人以上の人口で、市の中心地にその 6 割以上が居住し、また、商工業に関わる人たちやその家族の割合が人口の 6 割以上を占める地域を言います。

国と地方公共団体とは、国民や住民に必要な仕事を分担して行っています。

地方公共団体は、管轄する自治体の中の下水道、消防、学校、図書館、ごみ処理、高齢者福祉、産業の振興など、その地域の生活面、産業面に密着した部分を担っています。

地方公共団体は地方議会とよばれる議決機関とその議決機関の決定に基づいて実際の行政をすすめる執行機関とに分かれ、地方議会は都道府県議会と市町村議会とに分かれます。

地方議会では、その地方公共団体だけに適用される条例の制定・改正・廃止、予算の決定などを行い、執行機関は首長とよばれる都道府県知事、市町村長とその首長を助ける副知事、副市町村長の補助機関がおかれています。

地方公共団体では、議員も首長も住民の直接選挙で選ばれ、議会は一院制で任期は 4 年です。

Local Governance

Teacher

Today, we will learn about local self-government. We live in Tokyo, Japan.

Japan is divided into 47 prefectures, and each prefecture is subdivided into municipalities based on historical ties and the number of residents.

The occupations that operate according to these divisions are called public officials, and the representatives who reflect the ideas and opinions of the residents are called councilors and chiefs, who are elected by the residents to ensure that the majority of local opinions are reflected in the system.

Councilors and leaders are public servants, just like police officers and city hall employees. Local autonomy means that the residents living in each region independently manage the politics of that region, and the units that carry out that local autonomy are called local governments or municipality .

The criteria for a city are set in a law called the Local Autonomy Law, while the criteria for a town can be determined independently by the prefecture, and an area that falls under neither a city nor a town becomes a local public entity called a village.

A city is an area with a population of 50,000 or more, with 60% or more of that population living in the center of the city, and with people and their families involved in commerce and industry accounting for 60% or more of the population.

The national government and local governments share the work necessary for the people and residents.

Local governments are responsible for the parts of the local government under their jurisdiction that are closely related to the living and industrial aspects of the area, such as sewerage, firefighting, schools, libraries, waste disposal, welfare for the elderly, and promotion of industry.

Local public entities are divided into a voting body called a local assembly and an executive body that carries out actual administration based on the decisions of the voting body, and local assemblies are divided into prefectural and municipal assemblies.

The local assembly enacts, amends, or repeals ordinances applicable only to the local public entity, and decides on the budget. The executive branch consists of prefectural governors and municipal mayors, who are called chiefs, and vice governors and vice municipal mayors, who assist the chiefs, and their subsidiary bodies.

In local governments, councilors and mayors are directly elected by local residents, and councils are unicameral with a four-year term of office.

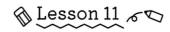

社会　Social Studies

国際連合と世界平和

高学年

先生

世界を巻き込んだ大きな戦争が2度も起き、平和と安全を守るために、当時の戦勝国であるアメリカやイギリスが中心となって1945年に成立されたのが国際連合です。

日本は1953年（昭和31年）に加盟しました。

国際連合には多くの機関があります。

総会は、全ての加盟国から代表者が集まる会議で、毎年1回、9月に開かれます。

国連教育科学文化機関（UNESCO ユネスコ）は、教育、科学、文化の発展による国際理解のもたらす平和を目的として設立されました。

まずしい国などで文字の読めない子たちに読み書きを教えて識字率（しきじりつ）を向上させる活動や、義務教育の普及のための活動、また、世界遺産の登録と保護などを行っています。

本部はフランスのパリです。

国際連合児童基金（UNICEF ユニセフ）は、戦争のある紛争地域など、めぐまれない環境の子供たちや、発展途上国）の子供たちを支援する活動をしています。

世界保健機関（WHO)は、感染病など病気の予防や対策を行ったり、世界の健康や衛生を守る仕事をしています。

国際通貨基金（IMF）は通貨の安定を目的とした機関です。

世界貿易機関（WTO)は、自由貿易をすすめるための機関です。

国連難民高等弁務官事務所（UNHCR）は、難民の保護と救済を目的に活動しています。

国際労働機関（ILO)は、世界の労働者の地位向上や労働条件の改善を目指す機関で、活動としては労働条件の最低条件を世界の各国に勧告しています。

国際原子力機関（IAEA)は、原子力の平和利用のための機関で、軍事利用を防ぐための査察などをしています。

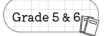

Grade 5 & 6

The United Nations and World Peace

Teacher

After two major wars involving the world, the United Nations was established in 1945, led by the United States and the United Kingdom, the victorious countries at that time, in order to protect peace and security.

Japan became a member in 1953.

The United Nations has many agencies.

The General Assembly, a meeting of representatives from all member countries, is held once a year in September.

The United Nations Educational, Scientific and Cultural Organization (UNESCO) was established to promote peace through international understanding by advancing education, science and culture.

UNESCO is responsible for improving literacy rates by teaching illiteracy to children in poor countries, promoting compulsory education, and registering and protecting World Heritage sites.

Its headquarters is in Paris, France.

United Nations Children's Fund (UNICEF) UNICEF works to support children in disadvantaged environments, such as war-torn conflict zones and children in developing countries.

The World Health Organization (WHO) works to prevent and combat infectious and other diseases and to protect global health and sanitation.

The International Monetary Fund (IMF) is responsible for currency stability.

The World Trade Organization (WTO) promotes free trade.

The United Nations High Commissioner for Refugees (UNHCR) works to protect and help refugees.

The International Labor Organization (ILO) works to improve the status and working conditions of workers around the world and recommends minimum working conditions to countries around the world.

The International Atomic Energy Agency (IAEA) is an organization for the peaceful use of nuclear energy and conducts inspections to prevent its military use.

ゴミという言葉

ゴミという言葉は、れっきとした日本語で、すでに、鎌倉時代の書物にも登場します。もともとは、主に農家で「木の葉」をあらわす言葉だったと言われています。

鎌倉前期の「平家物語」では「水田のごみ深かりける畔（あぜ）の上に」とあり、ドブなどに溜まる泥をさす言葉として使われており、ドブに溜まりやすいものの代表として、「木の葉」を意味していたとも考えられます。

ゴミという言葉が、「塵（ちり）」や「土ぼこり」のことをさすようになったのは近世以降で、その頃からゴミは不要な物であることから、「取るに足らないもの」「役に立たないもの」などの意味として使われはじめたようです。

ゴミ箱を護美箱と書いていることがありますが、この書き方は、おそらく1960年ごろに生まれたもののようです。『朝日新聞』の1962（昭和37）年12月10日付夕刊の「今日の問題」という記事よると、九州のある市で、市が「護美箱」と書いて規格品のゴミ箱を配ったところ、そんな仰々しい名前を付けるのはおこがましい、と批判が続出した、というのです。

「護美箱」は、漢文風に訓読すると「美を護（まも）る箱」となり、「ゴミを入れることにより周りの美しさを守る箱」という、ちょっとしゃれた当て字でした。

半世紀以上が過ぎ、最初は「仰々しい」と言われたこの書き方も、現在では、観光地や学校などで「護美箱」と書いたゴミ箱を見かけます。

ゴミに関する英語表現

ゴミを捨てるという英語表現

Throw away(out) the garbage
や
Dump the garbage

清掃業
Janitor
or
Cleaning business

一般ゴミ（主に紙切れや紙くず）
🇺🇸 Trash
🇬🇧 Rubbish

もともとは
生ゴミ（台所ゴミ）・一般ゴミ
🇺🇸 Garbage

ゴミ収集車
Garbage Truck (Wagon)

燃えるゴミ
Burnable Trash (Rubbish)

燃えないゴミ
Unburnable Trash (Rubbish)
or
Incombustibles

ゴミ箱
🇺🇸 Trash Can
🇬🇧 Rubbish Bin

外置きゴミ箱
Trash Containar
or
Dumpster

ゴミ捨て場
Trash Disposal
or
Garbage Dump

散乱したゴミ
（公共の場など）
Litter

（使用済み）廃棄物など
Waste

図工
subject 5

Arts and Crafts

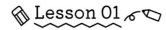
道具の使い方

 低学年

先生

1 図工の時間です。

2 時間割では、図工の時間は2時限続いています。

3 これは、図工の時間は、絵を書いたり、物を作ったりするので、時間がかかります。

4 それに、途中でやめて次の時間に続けて行うのが、難しいからです。

5 絵を描いたり、物を作ったりするのは楽しいし、面白いですよね。

6 皆さんも、小さいころから、楽しんできたと思います。

7 では、机の上に、道具箱を出して、開いてください。

8 何が入っているか、確認してみましょう。

9 1つ1つ確認しながら、道具箱から出して机の上に広げてみましょう。

10 次に、それぞれに自分の名前が書いてあるか、確認してください。

11 みんな同じものを持っていますから、名前が書いてないと、他の人のものと間違えたり、どこかに置き忘れたりしたときに、誰のものかわからなくなりますからね。

12 全部に、私たちの学校の『あざぶ2ちょうめしょうがっこう、1ねん2くみ』と書いてあるかも、確認してくださいね。

13 書き忘れていたら、手を挙げてください。

14 油性マジックペンがありますから、書いてあげますよ。

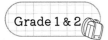

図工

Arts and Crafts

How to use Art Materials

Teacher

1. OK, it's time for art class.
2. On our timetable, we have the art class for two periods in a row.
3. That's because in art class, we draw and make things, which can take time.
4. Also, it's difficult to stop in the middle of a process and then start up again.
5. It's fun and interesting to draw a picture and make things, isn't it?
6. I'm sure all of you have enjoyed it since you were little.

7. Now, please get out and open up your art case on your desk.
8. Let's check what's inside.
9. One by one, take them out and put them on the desk.

10. Next, please make sure your names are written on each item.
11. We all have the same things so if your name isn't on it, it's going to be difficult to know whose it is if you misplace something.
12. Make sure our school's name, Azabu 2-chome Elementary School and your class is written on everything as well.
13. Please raise your hand if you forgot to write your name on something.
14. I have a permanent marker here so I can write it for you.

低学年

好きなものの絵を描こう

先生

1. 今日は、画用紙に、自分の好きなものを、クレパスで描きます。
2. 皆さん、クレパスを、道具箱から出してください。
3. クレパスを使ったことがありますか。
4. クレパスを使うときは、このように鉛筆を持つように持ちます。
5. 使った後は、出したところに戻してください。
6. 使った後、机の上に置いたままにすると、すぐに転がって、机から落ちてしまいます。

7. では、画用紙を配ります。
8. 一番前の人に列分を渡しますから、一枚ずつ取って、順番に後ろに回してください。
9. 一番後ろの人ももらいましたか。
10. 2枚持っている人はいませんか。
11. では、画用紙の表を、上にしてください。
12. どちらが表か裏か、わかる人いますか。
13. 画用紙の両面を指で触ってみて、そうしたら、わかるから。どうですか。
14. ツルツルした面と、ざらざらした面がありますね。
15. つるつるした方の面が、表です。表の面に描きます。

16. では、皆さん、描きはじめましょう。
17. クレパスの持ち方ですが、鉛筆と同じように持ちます。
18. 塗るときは、先に線で輪郭を描いてそれから中を塗るようにするときれいに塗れますよ。

19. 輪郭を描くときは、強く線を引いた方が、よいですね。その方が、その輪郭に沿って
20. はみ出ないように簡単に、色を塗ることができてきれいですよ。
21. クレパスやクレヨンは、鉛筆と違うから、消しゴムでは消せませんよ。
22. ほら、汚くなってしまいましたね。
23. そこは、白いパスで塗って、ぼかしてみて。
24. 線の内側の塗ったところに、隙間がありますね。
25. 隙間がないように、塗りつぶしてくださいね。

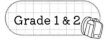

Grade 1 & 2

Draw your Favorite Things

Teacher

1. Today, we are going to use oil pastels and draw something you like on a drawing paper.
2. Everyone, take your out oil pastels.
3. Has everyone used these before?
4. The way to hold them is the same as how you hold a pencil.
5. After using it, you should put it back where it was.
6. If you leave it on the desk, it could easily roll on to the floor.

7. Now, I am going to hand out the papers for drawing.
8. I will give them to the person in the front row. Take one, and pass the rest back.
9. Has the person in the very back got one too?
10. Did anyone get two?
11. OK, now, place the paper with the front side up.
12. Does anybody know which side is front and which is back?
13. Now let's touch the paper and tell me what you can feel. How is it?
14. You can feel there is a smooth side and a rough side, right?
15. The smooth side is the front of the paper. You draw on that side.

16. Alright then, let's start drawing.
17. Hold the oil pastels like you hold a pencil.
18. I think when you color, you can color it nicely if you draw the outline first, and then color in the inside.
19. Press harder when you draw the outline so it's easier for you to follow, color carefully,
20. and try not to go outside of the lines so you can color it nicely.
21. Oil pastels and crayons are different from pencils so you can't use erasers if it gets messy.
22. You see, it has become dirty.
23. Use a white oil pastel over it and blend it in.
24. You can still see some spaces inside the outline.
25. Now try to use the whole sheet of paper.

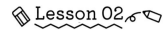 **Lesson 02**

図工

 低学年

すきなものの絵を描こう

先生

1　終わった人は、手にクレパスがついていないか確認して、手にクレパスがついていたら、後で石鹸で落としますから、今は雑巾でこすり落としておいてください。

2　皆さんも、道具箱から雑巾を出してくださいね。

3　はい、時間になりました。

4　皆さん、自分の描いた絵の裏に名前を書いて、持って、黒板の前に集まってください。

5　皆さんの作品を黒板に貼りますからね。

6　では、自分の席に戻って、片づけを始めてください。何度もいいますが、クレパスは、ちゃんとパスの箱に、同じ向きに入れてから、

7　道具箱にしまってください。

8　雑巾もしまってください。皆さん、しまいましたか。

9　しまったら、机の中に入れて、廊下に並んでください。

10　手を洗いに行きますよ。

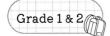

Grade 1 & 2

Draw your Favorite Things

Teacher

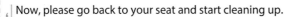

☐ Those of you who are finished, check if you have pastel on your hands and if you do,

1 then you can wash them with soap later. For now, just rub it off using your rag.

2 Please get your art rags out from your case.

3 OK, time's up.

4 Write your name on the back of the paper, bring it forward, and gather at the blackboard.

5 I am going to display your drawings on the black board.

6 Now, please go back to your seat and start cleaning up.

  Like I said many times before, you must put the oil pastels back where they were in

7 the same direction, OK?

8 Please put the box back in the case. Same for the rag.

9 OK, is everyone done, Now, put the case back in your desk and line up in the hallway.

10 We are off to wash our hands.

Art
♂

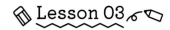
低学年

ハサミをつかってみよう

先生

1　道具箱から、はさみと糊を出してください。

2　今日は、はさみと糊を使って、いろんなものを切ったり、張り付けて作ったりして工作をします。

3　はさみは、カッターや包丁と同じく、刃物といって、危ない道具です。

4　ふざけて振り回したり、お友達の方に刃先を向けたりしてはいけません。

5　友達に渡すときは、柄の方を向けて渡し、刃を相手に向けて渡してはいけません。

6　では、色紙を配ります。

7　第1班の人は、色紙の辺と辺を合わせて、長方形をつくって、半円に切ってください。

8　第2班の人は、角と角を合わせて、三角形を作って、もう一回折って、そのくっついているところを残して、真ん中を切ってみてください。

9　第3班の人は、色紙を丸めて筒のようにして、筒の上と下に4か所ずつ、切れ目を入れてください。

10　色紙を切るときは、根元まで紙を差し込んで、ゆっくりと切ってください。

Grade 1 & 2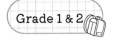

Let's Use Scissors

Teacher

1 Please take out your scissors and a glue.

2 Today, we will use scissors and glue to cut and glue various things together to make crafts.

3 Scissors, like cutters and knives, are dangerous tools.

4 So, never fool around by swinging them around or pointing them towards people.

When you pass them, give them the handle side. Never pass them with the blade

5 side pointing to the person.

6 Now, I'm going to give out some origami paper.

Group 1 students, put both sides of the origami paper together and fold it in half to make

7 them into a rectangle and cut out a half circle.

Group 2 students, put both angles of the origami paper together and fold it to make a triangle

8 then fold again and cut the middle.

Group 3, I want you to roll the paper like a tube then add four small cuts at the top and bottom

9 of the tube.

10 When you cut the paper, make sure you insert the paper all the way and cut them slowly.

低学年

粘土工作

先生

1 粘土を両手で丸めてください。

2 粘土を細長くしてください。

3 端をちぎって、そのちぎった粘土を、元の粘土にくっつけてください。

4 粘土は、自由に形を変えることができます。

5 これを使って、今日は工作をします。

6 では、粘土で、動物園にいる動物を作ってみましょう。

7 作りたい動物がどんな形か、よくわからないときは、本棚の動物図鑑を見てください。

8 濡らした雑巾を準備します。

粘土が乾きすぎると固くなり動物が作りつらくなりますから、そのときは雑巾で包んで

9 濡らすと柔らかくなって使いやすくなります。

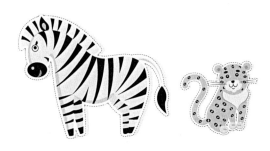

Creating with Clay

Grade 1 & 2

Teacher

1 Please roll the clay with both hands.

2 Make the clay long and thin.

3 Tear off the ends and attach the torn clay back on to the original clay.

4 Clay can be changed into shape like.

5 Today, we are going to use the clay to make things.

6 Now, let's make some animals at a zoo with clay .

If you are not sure what shape the animal you want to make is, look at the animal book on

7 the bookshelf.

8 Prepare a wet rag.

When the clay gets too dry, it will harden and it will be difficult to shape the animal.

When that happens, cover the clay with the wet rag. Then, the clay will become softer and

9 will be easier for you to manage.

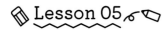

低学年

三原色を知ろう

先生

1　皆さんのクレパスと絵の具の箱を見てください。

　大体、絵の具やクレパスは、12色あるいは24色入りが多いですが、実は、たった3色で、

2　これらの色が作られていることを知っていますか。

3　赤色、黄色、青色の三色があると、すべての色が作れるんですよ。

4　今日は、みんなで、いろんな色を作ることに挑戦してみましょう。

5　絵の具を使います。

6　では、皆さん準備しましょう。

　絵の具は、チューブに入っていて、チューブからパレットに絵の具を出して、

7　水と筆を使います。

8　手洗い場から、水入れを運んでくるとき、水がこぼれないように、気をつけてください。

9　もし、水をこぼしてしまうことがあったら、雑巾で、床を拭いてください。

10　水をこぼしたり、絵の具で机が汚れないように、新聞紙で机を覆うことにしましょう。

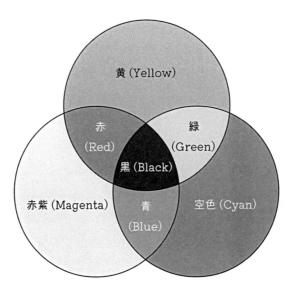

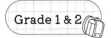 Grade 1 & 2

Let's Learn about Primary Colors

Teacher

1. Everyone, take a look at your boxes of crayons and paints.

Most have 12, and some have 24 colors. But actually, do you know that those colors are made

2. from 3 colors?

3. With three colors, red, yellow, and blue, you can make all the colors.

4. Today let's try to make different colors.

5. We are going to use paints.

6. OK, let's get ready.

The paints come in tubes, so you need to squeeze the paints out of the tubes onto a palette

7. and use water and a brush.

8. When you bring the water container from the washroom, be careful not to spill the water.

9. If you happen to spill water, please wipe the floor with a rag.

10. Cover the desk with newspaper to prevent water spills and paint from staining the desk.

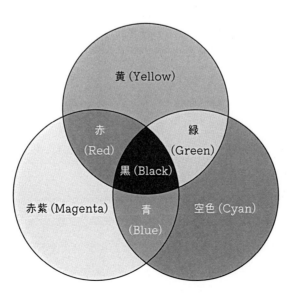

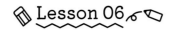

たなばたかざりを作ろう

先生

1 もうすぐ、七夕ですね。七夕の時に、笹の葉に飾るものは何ですか。

2 たんざくです。そうですね。

3 短冊にお願いごとを書いて飾ります。短冊は、いろんな色があります。

4 今回は、3原色を学習して色を作ることに興味がわいてきたと思います。

5 今度は、自分で作った色の短冊を作ってみましょう。

6 そして、短冊にお願いことを書きましょう。きっと叶いますよ。

7 では、机を班ごとに、向い合わせにしてください。

8 その上を、新聞で覆ってください。

9 1枚を広げると薄いですから、2枚重ねて、覆ってください。

10 机全体を覆って、新聞紙と新聞紙の間に、隙間がないようにしてくださいね。

11 机が離れていると、隙間ができて、絵の具や水差しが落ちますからね。

12 各班の班長は、教壇まで、班の人数分の紙ナプキンを取りに来てください。

13 各班の男の子は、水入れに、水を汲んできてください。

14 各班の女の子は、紙コップと食紅を取りに来てください。

15 全員、座ってください。

16 では、初めに、紙ナプキンを半分に折り、長方形の形にして、さらに、もう1度折って、細長い長方形にしてください。

17 出来ましたね。そしたら、細長くなったナプキンの両端を中心線に向かって折り、さらに半分に折り、小さな正方形を作ってください。

18 紙ナプキンは破れやすいから、みんな優しく扱ってね。

19 そろそろいいですか。

20 そしたら、ナプキンの角を一か所ずつ、三つの色に浸していってください。

21 4つの角を浸し終わったら、破れないように、ゆっくりと、紙ナプキンを広げてみてください。

22 ほら、色がまじりあって、グラデーションになっているでしょ！

23 では、それを明日まで、干して乾かしましょう。

　順番に持ってきてください。窓のところの洗濯ロープに、洗濯バサミで留めます。

24 誰の紙ナプキンかわからなくなりますから、班ごとに、洗濯ばさみの色を変えますよ。

Creating Tanabata Decorations

Teacher

1. Tanabata festival is coming soon. Do you know what we hang on the bamboo leaves?

2. It's tanzaku, right?

3. We write our wishes on tanzaku strips and decorate them. Tanzakus come in various colors.

4. Since we learned the primary colors, you must be excited to use colors now.

5. Now, let's start making your own original tanzaku using your own colors.

6. Then write your wish on it. I'm sure your wish will come true!

7. Now, please put your desks facing each other in groups.

8. And, cover your desks with newspaper.

9. It will be too thin to use one sheet, so use two sheets to cover them.

10. Make sure all the desks are covered with no empty space, okay?

11. If the desks have any spaces in between them, the paints or the water buckets can spill.

12. The leader of each group, please come up and take paper napkins.

13. Boys of each group, please collect water in the paint bucket.

14. Girls of each group, please come and get the paper cups and food coloring.

15. Everybody please sit down.

16. Firstly, please fold the paper napkin into half, and make a rectangle, then fold it once again to make a thinner rectangle.

17. Great, now bring both ends to the center of the thinner rectangle and fold it in half to make a small square.

18. Paper napkins easily get ripped, so handle them gently, okay?

19. I think they're all ready now.

20. Now, dip the corners of the paper napkin one at a time in to the three colors.

21. After you finish dipping all four corners, gently open the paper napkin, being careful not to rip it.

22. See how the colors are mixed and it has a gradation!

23. Now, we'll let these dry out until tomorrow.

24. Please bring them over one at a time. I am going to dry them by hanging them on a clothes line with pegs. Each group will use a different color clothes peg so we don't get mixed up.

低学年

たなばたかざりを作ろう

先生

1 先週作った染めたナプキンを使って、短冊をつくります。

2 自分のナプキンを持ってきてください。

3 では、机の上に新聞を広げて、その上に、ナプキン、糊、はさみ、サインペンを載せて ください。

4 いいですか。

5 皆さんが染めたナプキンを、前回と同じように、長方形に2回折って、それを広げて、折り目をはさみで切ってください。

6 全員、4本の短冊が出来ましたね。

7 そのまま、願いごとを書いてもよいのですが、もうすこしやってみましょう。

8 では、それぞれの短冊を星形やひし形、丸形などを切り抜いて、それを貼り付けて素敵な短冊を作りましょう。

9 はさみを使って、考えている形を切り抜くのは難しいですね。

10 なので、形を短冊に鉛筆で書いてみてください。

11 丸い形や、三角形などの形を書くのは 難しいですね。

12 身の回りの物を使って、好きな形をなぞりさます。

13 それを切り取って、糊で貼りつけてから、自分だけの短冊を作り、それに願いごとを書いてください。

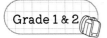
Creating Tanabata Decorations

Grade 1 & 2

Teacher

1. We are going to make tanzaku with the paper napkin we dyed last week.

2. Please collect your own napkin.

3. Now, please spread out newspaper and put your napkin, glue, scissors and a marker on top of it.

4. Ok, everyone.

   Fold your dyed napkin two times like last time, then, open it up and cut the folded part with

5. scissors.

6. Everyone now has 4 tanzaku, right?

7. We could write our wish now, but let's do some more.

   Now, cut out a star, a diamond, a circle, etc. from each strip of paper, and paste them together

8. to make a beautiful strip of paper.

9. It's hard to cut out the shapes you are thinking of with scissors.

10. So, try to draw the shapes on the tanzaku with a pencil.

11. It's difficult to draw round shapes, and triangular shapes, right?

12. Use anything around you to trace any shapes you wish.

13. Then, cut them out, and glue them. Make an original tanzaku and write your wish on it !

低学年

風船をファンシーボールに変身させよう

先生

1 今日は、風船を変身させます。

2 こちらが、皆さんが知っている風船です。

3 そしてこちらが変身した風船です。すてきでしょう！

4 今日は、風船を変身させて楽しみます。

5 いくつか、変身した風船を持ってきましたから、班で、よく観察してみてください。

6 大切なことは、どのようにして、風船をこんなきれいに、変身させたかです。

7 何を付けたんだろう、何を使ったんだろうを見てください。

8 では、はじめる準備をしますよ。

9 新聞紙を２枚、風船１個、色薄紙３枚と、糊１個、リボン１本と飾り、紙箱を座席順に取りに来て、机の上においてください。

10 道具箱から雑巾と筆を出して、雑巾は、濡らしてきてください。

11 そこまでいいですか。

12 では、次に、新聞紙と薄紙を、細長くちぎってください。

13 新聞紙と薄紙が、混じらないようにしてください。

14 先に、新聞紙で風船を包みますからね。

15 ハサミで切らないで、手でちぎったほうが、後で風船によくつきます。

16 はい、では、容器に糊を入れて、水で溶かしてください。筆でぐるぐる回して。

17 これで糊の準備ができましたね。

18 では、風船を膨らませます。風船を膨らませたことありますね。

19 風船を何回か、いろいろな方向から引っ張って柔らかくしてください。

20 初めに伸ばしておくと、後で、口で膨らませるときに楽です。

21 いろいろな方向に引っ張るときに、風船を破かないように気を付けましょうね。

22 強くひっぱりすぎると、空気を入れたときに、穴が開いてしまうことがあります。

23 少し引っ張るだけで大丈夫ですよ！

24 人差し指と親指で、吹き口をつまんでくださいね。

25 そしたら、風船に息を吹きこんでください。

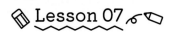
Grade 1 & 2

Let's Transform a Balloon into a Fancy Ball

Teacher

1 We are going to transform a balloon today.

2 This is an ordinary balloon that you all know.

3 And this is what I transformed it into. It's nice, isn't it?

4 Today, I want you to enjoy transforming a balloon into a fancy ball.

5 I brought a few balloons here that have already been transformed, so please observe them carefully in your group.

6 The important thing to discuss is how the balloons were transformed into such beautiful balloons.

7 Look carefully at what they added and what they used.

8 Now, let's get ready to start.

Please come up in your seated order and get 2 pieces of newspaper, 1 balloon, 3 assorted art tissues, 1 bottle of glue, a ribbon and some decorations.

9 Put them on your desk when you have collected them.

10 Get a rag and a brush from the toolbox and wet the rag.

11 Is everyone OK so far?

12 Now, I want you to tear the newspaper and art tissue into strips.

13 Please don't mix the newspaper and the art tissue together.

14 We will first cover the balloon with the newspaper.

15 Tearing the newspaper into strips instead of cutting them will allow us to lay them flatter on the balloon.

16 Now, put some glue into the container and add some water to dilute it with a brush.

17 Now we are set for gluing.

18 Now, inflate the balloon. You have inflated balloons before, right?

19 Loosen the balloon by stretching it in all directions.

20 If you stretch out the balloon first, it becomes much easier to blow up with your mouth afterwards.

21 Stretch the balloon in all directions, being careful not to rip the balloon.

22 Just make sure not to stretch the balloon too much, or it might pop when you inflate it.

23 A few stretches here and there will get the job done!

24 Pinch the neck of the balloon with your index finger and thumb.

25 Then blow air into the balloon.

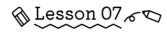
風船をファンシーボールに変身させよう

 低学年

先生

1 最後は、空気が出ないように、下の部分を結びます。

2 どうやってやるかというと、左の親指と人差し指で押さえている間に、右手で先端部を引っ張って、結び目をつくります。

3 さっきちぎった新聞を、先ほど作った糊につけてください。

4 新聞についた余計な糊は、垂れてこないように、親指と人差し指で挟んで、取り除きましょうね。

5 では、次に、風船に新聞全体に貼っていきます。

6 どんどんいろいろな方向から貼って、風船が見えなくなるまで続けてください。

7 後で、風船をとるために、風船の結び目のところの小さな部分は、貼らないでね。

8 風船が、新聞紙で見えなくなったら、その新聞紙の上に、ちぎった薄紙を貼っていってください。違う色の薄紙を順番に貼ったり、縦から貼ったり、横から貼ったりして、何回か重ねて、風船が見えないように貼っていってください。

9 終わったら、完全に乾かせます。

10 乾いてから、中の風船を割って、割れた風船を、さっきの穴から引き出します。

11 リボンを風船の結び目に巻いて、指が通るようにしてください。

12 完成しましたか。

13 完成したら、友達がどんなファンシーボールを使ったか、見てみましょうね。

14 順番に、前に出て、自分の作品をみんなに見せて、気に入っているところ、今日の感想とかを発表してください。

15 皆の作品の紹介が終わったら、糊を乾燥させるために、洗濯ロープに、ぶら下げます。家に持って帰るのは、明日になります。

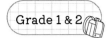
Let's Transform a Balloon into a Fancy Ball

Teacher

1 The final step is to tie the bottom up so that no air comes out.

To do this, you should hold the bottom using your left thumb and index finger while stretching

2 the very end with your right hand to make a knot.

3 Dip the newspaper strips into the paste you made.

Remove any extra glue on the newspaper strips by running it through your pinched fingers,

4 okay?

5 Spread and paste the newspaper onto the balloon.

Continue doing so, making the strips go in all different directions until your balloon is

6 completely covered.

Make sure you leave a small hole at the end where the balloon is tied so you can remove

7 the balloon.

After you completely covered the balloon with newspaper, start pasting stripes of assorted

art tissue in all directions again until your balloon is completely covered. Add two or three

8 more layers to your balloon.

9 When you are done, let it dry completely.

10 Once it is dry, pop the balloon and remove it through the opening you left.

I want you to use the ribbon to tie the knot of the balloon and make a loop so you can put

11 your finger through it.

12 Are you done?

13 If you are done, let's see everyone's fancy balls.

Everyone comes up to the front one at a time and tell us about it. Show your fancy ball and

14 share with the class the areas you like and what you thought about today's class, OK?

After everyone is done sharing, then we will hang your fancy balls on the rope overnight so

15 they will get completely dry. You can take them home tomorrow.

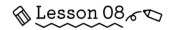
糸巻きスーパーカー

 低学年

先生

今日は、みんな、割りばしと輪ゴムと糸巻き、輪切りにしたローソク、紙コップ、セロテープは持ってきましたね。今日は、ゴムで走るスーパーカーを作ります。

誰のスーパーカーが速いか、競争します!

まず、割りばしの細い方を、2㎝くらいのところで、折ってください。

次に、輪ゴムを割りばしに通し、ろうそくの穴を通し、それを、糸巻きの穴から入れて、反対の穴から輪ゴムの先を引き出して、さっき折った割りばしの端を通して、

輪ゴムを通したら、その割りばしの端を、セロテープで留めてください。

はい、全員、車輪は出来上がりましたね。では、次に、紙コップを出してください。

紙コップの上の部分を、少し切り取りますよ。

定規と鉛筆を出して、コップの口から2㎝のところを、定規で測って、そこまで線を引いて、そのあと、横に2.5㎝くらいのところに、同じく2㎝の線を、引いてください。

割りばし車輪が、通るところになります。

線を引いたら、はさみで切ってください。

気を付けてね。紙コップは弱いから、手で強く押さえると、そこのところがつぶれてしまって、スーパーカーが作れません。

つぶれないように気を付けて、ゆっくりと、はさみで切り取りますよ。

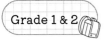 Grade 1 & 2

Let's Make a super car from a spool of thread!

Teacher

Today, everyone brought a chopstick, rubber band, a spool of thread, pre-cut candle,

a paper cup, and a tape, right? Today, we are going to make a car powered with a rubber band.

We are going to compete to see whose car runs the fastest!

First, I want you to split the thinner part of your chopsticks to around 2cm from the end.

Next, put the rubber band through the chopsticks and then put it through the candle too.

And from that, take out the thread from the opposite side. Bring the thread back to

the split side of the chopsticks through the rubber band and close off the chopsticks with tape.

OK, everyone has their own wheels, right? Now, please take out the paper cup.

You should cut the top of the cup just a little bit.

Please take out a ruler and a pencil to draw a line 2cm from the top. And then,

at about 2.5cm on the side of that line, draw another 2cm.

Those are the lines where the wheels will go.

After you draw the lines, use scissors to cut the lines.

Be careful, because these cups are very soft. If you hold it too strong, you will squish them and

you won't have a nice supercar.

You can do it slowly so that it won't be squished.

糸巻きスーパーカー

先生

1. では、紙コップを、糸巻の上にかぶせてみてください。
2. 穴をあけた部分の位置を確認してください。では、その紙コップに、好きな絵を描いてください。
3. 絵を描くのは、サインペンにします。パスや絵の具は、使わないでください。
4. 絵の具は、水で溶かしていますので、紙は濡れると柔らかくなり、破れやすくなります。
5. だから、サインペンを使います。

6. コップは丸いですね。
7. これまで描いていたのは、画用紙でしたから、丸いものに描くのは初めてですね。
8. コップの前の部分だけでなく、横と後ろも描きます。
9. 前に授業でやった、粘土で動物園の動物をどう作ったか思い出してください。
10. 前からだけでなく、後ろからみたとき、横から見たときを考えながら、作りましたね。

11. あの時と同じです。
12. どうしても思い出せない人は、教室の前の壁にある、こけし人形を見に来てください。

13. サインペンに注意してね。
14. サインペンは、手や洋服に付けると、取れなくなってしまいます。
15. お洋服は、袖口が長いから、肘のあたりまで、腕まくりした方がいいですね。
16. 出来上がったら、輪ゴムをまいて、みんなでレースしますよ。

Grade 1 & 2

Let's Make a super car from a spool of thread!

Teacher

1 | Let's now put the cup up on the thread.

2 | Thinking about where the hole is, you can draw whatever pictures you want to draw on it.

3 | Let's use a pen to draw, not a crayon or paint.

4 | Also, paint contains water, so the paper cup won't be able to hold up.

5 | That's why we are using a pen.

6 | You see, a cup is round.

7 | So far, we have only drawn on flat paper, but this time it's on a rounded surface.

8 | You can not only draw on the front but also on the sides as well as the back.

9 | Remember when we made animals from clay?

We not only thought about how it looks from the front but also from the back as well as from

10 | the side.

11 | It's the same this time, too.

If you can't remember what to do, you can come and look at the example at the front of

12 | the classroom as many times as you like.

13 | Be careful with the pens though.

14 | You can't get rid of the mark if you draw on your clothes.

15 | If your clothes have long cuffs, you should roll it up to your elbows.

16 | Well, once everyone finishes, we will have a race.

Art
of

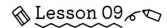
中学年

段ボール工作

先生

今日は、文化祭の出し物「魚釣り名人」のセットを作りましょう。

まず、段ボールでつくるものが一番大変そうですから、これから準備しましょう。

では、段ボールはどういう素材で、どういうことができるか、どういうことに気をつけないといけないかを考えます。

段ボールは、紙ですが板のように固いので、丈夫ですが、切ったり曲げたりするのが大変です。

段ボールと厚紙は、どう違うかわかりますか。

段ボールの厚さの部分を見てください。

2枚の紙の間に波状の紙を挟んで丈夫さを強化したものです。

これは段ボールの中にあった仕切り板です。

これも段ボールでできています。

両方の段ボールに切り込みを入れて、切り込みの部分を差し込んで組み合わせてありますね。

こちらの段ボールを見てください。

これは段ボールの底です。4枚の底板を片方ずつ重ねて、テープも使わずに開かないようにしてあります。

板みたいに固いけど、やっぱり紙なので、切りやすいし、曲げることもできるという段ボールの特長を生かしています。

段ボールを切断するときは、できるだけ、折り目のところに段ボールカッターを当てて切ります。

一回に切ろうとして力を入れると危ないので、何回も刃を当てて、少しずつ切ってください。

段ボールは、絵の具は塗りにくいですが、マジックやチョークは書きやすいので、上手に丸が書けると思います。

段ボールを切り抜くときは、大きめのはさみで切り抜いていきますが、かなり力を入れないと、はさみが切れないので注意してくださいね。

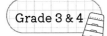

Cardboard Craft

Teacher

1 Today, let's make a set for the "Fishing Master" program of the school festival.

First of all, let's prepare what we are going to make out of cardboard, because it seems to

2 be the most difficult thing to make.

Now, let's consider what kind of material cardboard is, what it is able to do, and what we

3 need to be careful of.

4 Cardboard is paper but hard like a board, so it is strong also it's difficult to cut and bend.

5 Do you know what the difference is between cardboard box and cardboard paper?

6 Look at the thickness of the cardboard.

7 Wavy paper is sandwiched between two sheets of paper to strengthen its durability.

8 This is a divider board found inside a cardboard box.

9 This is also made of cardboard.

A slit is cut in both pieces of cardboard and the slits are inserted into each other to combine

10 them.

11 See the cardboard here.

This is the bottom of a cardboard box, with four bottom boards stacked one on top of the other,

12 so that it won't open without any tape.

13 It is hard like a slice of wood, but it is still paper, so it is easy to cut or bend.

14 This is a special characteristic of cardboard.

15 When cutting cardboard, place the cardboard cutter at the folds and cut, as much as possible.

If you try to cut it all at once with too much pressure, it will be dangerous, so apply the cutter

16 several times and cut it gradually.

Cardboard is difficult to paint on, but magic markers and chalk are easy to write with,

17 so you can draw good circles on it.

When cutting through the cardboard, use large scissors to cut through the cardboard,

18 but be careful because you have to use a lot of pressure to cut through with the scissors.

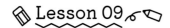
中学年

段ボール工作

先生

1 文化祭の準備で使った段ボールが余りましたね。では、余った段ボールを使って

2 面白いものを作ってみましょう。

3 各班で、ひと箱ずつ段ボールを持って行ってください。

4 ミカン箱くらいの段ボールがよいです。

そしたら、半径5cmほどの円をコンパスで、狭い方の横板に描きます。

5 その円をくりぬいて下さい。

6 くりぬくときは、段ボールカッターで何度も少しずつ刃を当てて切っていきます。

7 一気にくり抜こうとしないでください。円を切り抜くのは、難しいわね。

切り抜きやすいように、段ボールの切り抜くところを少しずつ回して、自分の正面に

8 もってくると力が入れやすいですよ。

9 各班、くりぬけましたか。

10 そしたら、箱のすべての隙間をガムテープで密閉してください。

11 外側からだけでなく、できるだけ、内側からも貼ってください。

12 出来ましたね。

13 いまから、線香に火をつけて配りますから、

14 線香の煙を穴から段ボールの中に入れてください。

15 煙は上に立ち上ります。

16 だから、線香の入ったアルミ缶の上に団ポールの穴を空いた側をかざしますよ。

17 煙が充満するまでしばらくかざしてきてください。

18 はい、煙が充満しましたか。

19 それでは、穴の開いてる方を前に向けて、机の上にのせてください。

20 準備はできましたか。

21 では、団ポール箱の横を両手でバンと叩いてください。

22 煙の輪が出てきましたね。

23 はい、もう1回たたいてみてください。

24 出なくなったら、また線香の煙を充満してやってください。

25 楽しいでしょ。

26 なぜ、空気でローソクが消せたんですか。

27 段ボールの中には、その大きさの分の空気が入っていますね。

両手でたたくと、たたいたところの段ボールが狭くなりますで、だから、空気が開いてる

28 穴からいきよいよく飛び出してきたんです。

図工

Grade 3 & 4

Cardboard Craft

Teacher

1 | You have leftover cardboard from the preparation for the festival.

2 | Now, let's make something interesting with them.

3 | Each group should take one box of cardboard boxes each.

4 | A cardboard box about the size of a tangerine box is best.

5 | Then, using a compass, draw a circle with a radius of about 5 cm on the narrower side of the cardboard. Hollow out that circle.

6 | When hollowing out the cardboard, use a cardboard cutter to cut by applying the blade little by little over and over again.

7 | Do not try to hollow it out all at once. Is it difficult to cut out a circle shape?

8 | To make it easier to cut out, turn the cardboard cutout little by little and place it in front of you so that it is easier to apply force.

9 | Has each group finished hallowing out their circle?

10 | Then, seal all gaps in the box with duct tape.

11 | Please apply the tape not only from the outside, but also from the inside as much as possible.

12 | You have done it, right?

13 | Now, I will light the incense sticks and distribute them.

14 | Please let the smoke from the incense stick go through the hole into the cardboard.

15 | The smoke will rise upwards.

16 | So, hold the side with the hole in the cardboard, over the aluminum can containing the incense.

17 | Go ahead and hold it up for a while until the smoke fills it up.

18 | Yes, has it filled up with smoke?

19 | Now, please place it on the table with the hole facing forward.

20 | Are you ready?

21 | Now, please tap the side of the cardboard box with both hands.

22 | You've made a smoke ring, haven't you.

23 | Yes, try tapping it again.

24 | When they stop, please fill them with incense smoke again.

25 | It's fun, isn't it?

26 | Why was the candle extinguished by air?

27 | The cardboard has air in it to fill it to its size.

28 | When you hit it with both hands, the cardboard becomes narrow at the point where you hit it, so the air comes out of the open hole with great force.

親子工作

中学年

先生

1 本日は、お忙しい中、授業参観にお越しいただきありがとうございます。

学年が上がるに従い、子どもたちの学習範囲も広くなるともに、経験する事柄も
2 多くなってきます。

今日は、事前にご連絡しましたように、社会科で学習した「昔の遊びを知ろう」の体験と
3 理科的要素も含んで、「竹の紙鉄砲」の工作に取り組みたいと思います。

4 材料が竹ですので、工作中に、とげが指に刺さることもあります。

5 必ずお持ちいただいている軍手を着用してください。

また、筒を作るために、竹を切断するのこぎりと表面を整えるための小刀を使いますが、

なかなかご自宅でこれらの道具を使う機会もなくなっており、使い方を知らないお子さんも
6 多いので、今日は保護者の方が主に行ってください。

7 まず、初めに、竹筒を作ります。鉄砲の銃身の部分です。

8 竹の中は節と節の間が空洞となっています。

9 節と節の間をのこぎりで切って、筒を作ってください。

10 なお、竹は根元の方が太くなっています。

11 厚みもありますので、根元の方の節を切ってください。

竹は丸くなっていますから、のこぎりの歯を立てると、ぐるぐる回転して切ることが
12 できませんし、のこぎりが滑って危険です。

13 のこぎりで切る人以外は、竹が回転しないようにしっかり押さえてください。

14 筒の長さは約15㎝とします。定規で測って印をつけてください。

竹を切るときは、切る部分をまず握り、その握ったところに沿った部分にのこぎりの歯を
15 当て、小刻みにのこぎりを動かして切っていきます。

切り出したら、竹を持っている人は竹を少し下に押さえ、切り口が開くようにすると切り
16 やすくなります。

17 切断できたら、小刀で切り口の繊維を削って形を整えてください。

18 次に押し棒を作ります。

19 押し棒は、筒の中で弾を押す役割ですが、当然、そのままだと筒の中で滑って押せませんね。

20 押し棒の取っ手を作る必要があります。

21 取っ手は、筒を切り取った竹の残りの部分を使いますが、片方は節を残してください。

22 そうしないと押し棒の取っ手になりません。

23 取っ手は手で握れるように約10㎝の長さで切ってください。

Parent and Child Crafts

Teacher

1. Thank you for taking time out of your busy schedule today to visit our class.

   As children move up through the grades, the scope of their studies becomes broader and they
2. experience more and more things.

   Today, as we previously announced, we would like to work on a "bamboo paper gun" craft, which includes both the experience of "Let's learn about old games" learned in social studies
3. and a scientific component.
4. Since the material is bamboo, thorns may prick your fingers during the crafting process.
5. Please be sure to wear your own work gloves.

   To make the tube, we also use a saw to cut the bamboo and a small knife to prepare the surface.

   However, since the opportunity to use these tools at home is not readily available and many
6. children do not know how to use them, parents should be the main ones to do this today.
7. First, at the beginning, we will make a bamboo tube. This is the barrel of a gun.
8. Inside the bamboo, there is hollow space between the joints.
9. Cut the space between the joints with a saw to make a cylinder.
10. Bamboo is thicker at the base.
11. Since it is thicker, please cut off the knot at the base.

    The Bamboo is rounded, so if you set the saw's teeth on it, it will spin around and you won't
12. be able to cut it, and the saw will slip, which is dangerous.
13. Only the person cutting with the saw should hold the bamboo firmly so that it does not rotate.
14. The length of the tube should be approximately 15 cm. Measure and mark with a ruler.

    When you're cutting the bamboo, first grip the part to be cut, then apply the teeth of the saw to
15. the area along the grip, and cut by moving the saw little by little.

    Once the bamboo is cut, the person holding the bamboo should hold it down slightly so that
16. the cut end opens up, making it easier to cut.
17. Once you cut, use a small knife to shave the cut fibers to shape it.
18. Next, we will make the push stick.

    The push stick is responsible for pushing the bullet inside the cylinder, but of course,
19. if it is left in place, it will slide inside the cylinder and cannot be pushed.
20. You need to make a handle for the push rod.

    For the handle, use the remaining part of the bamboo from which the tube was cut,
21. but leave one of the joints.
22. Otherwise, it will not become the handle for a push stick.
23. The handle should be cut about 10 cm long so that it can be held by hand.

ソーラーカーを作ろう

中学年

先生

1　理科で、電池のことを学習しましたから、実際に、太陽の光を電池エネルギーに変えて、

2　モーターを動かしたり、豆電球を光らせたりすることができるのかを実験してみましょう。

　折角、モーターを動かせるかを実験するのですから、太陽電池とモーターを搭載した

3　ソーラーカーを作って実験してみましょう。

　部品集めから行い、ソーラーカーすべてを手作りでできたらもっと楽しいと思うのですが、

4　今回は、組み立てよりも太陽電池の働きの確認をしたいのでキットで組み立てます。

5　小さな部品もありますから、無くならないように机に新聞紙を敷いてください。

6　良いですか。今からキットと道具を配ります。

7　ドライバーとニッパです。

8　まず、キットの中から、太陽電池とモーターを取り出してください。

9　そしたら、太陽電池とモーターをつないでみてください。

10　コードの色は関係ありませんよ。結びましたね。

11　はい、みんなで窓のところにそれをもってきて、太陽に電池を向けてみてください。

12　モーターが動きましたか？

13　はい、では席に戻って、組み立て説明書を開いてください。

14　最初のページにパーツリストが載っていますね。

15　班長が確認して、書記がそのリストの□に部品があるかをチェックして下さい。

16　次のページを開いて組み立てを始めてください。

17　とくに、モーターの取り付けとギアの取付けは、図面をよく見てやってください。

　ギアのことについては上級生になってから学習しますが、歯車といって、大きなギザギザに

18　なっていて、これを噛み合わせて、回転をさせてきます。

　実際の車にもエンジンというモーターから車輪までは同じように歯車でモーターの回転が

19　伝わるようになっています。

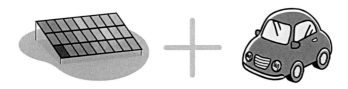

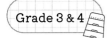
Grade 3 & 4

Let's make a solar car!

Teacher

1 Since we learned about batteries in science class, let's experiment to see if we can actually

2 convert sunlight into battery energy to run a motor or make a miniature light bulb glow.

And since we are going to experiment to see if we can run a motor, let's build a solar car

3 equipped with solar cells and a motor and conduct the experiment.

I think it would be more fun if we could collect the parts and make the entire solar car by hand,

but this time, I would rather assemble the car from a kit to check how the solar cells work than

4 assemble it.

5 Some parts are small, so please spread newspaper on your desk so that you don't lose them.

6 OK. I'm going to hand out the kits and tools now.

7 Here are the screwdrivers and the nippers.

8 First, remove the solar cell and motor from the kit.

9 Then try to connect the solar cell to the motor.

10 It doesn't matter what color the cord is. Tie them together, okay?

11 OK, now everyone brings it to the window and point the battery at the sun.

12 Did the motor start?

13 So, now please return to your seat and open the assembly instructions.

14 You see a parts list on the first page.

15 The group leader should check it and the secretary should check if there is a part in □ on that list.

16 Open the next page to begin assembly.

17 Especially, pay close attention to the drawings for the installation of the motor and gears.

You will learn about gears in your senior year, but they are gears with big jagged edges that

18 mesh together to make them rotate.

In actual cars, the rotation of the motor is transmitted from the motor, the engine,

19 to the wheels by gears in the same way.

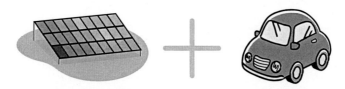

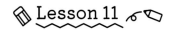
中学年

ソーラーカーを作ろう

先生

1 組み立て説明書③に書いてありますが、ギアの向きを間違えないでください。

2 それと説明書⑤に書いてあるネジ留めですね。

ドライバーを使ってネジを留めるものも初めてでしょうが、やったことがある人が

3 中心となってうまく回してください。

4 ネジ穴に入れて少し指で回さないと、ネジがネジ穴から落ちてしまいます。

ドライバーで回すときもネジが小さいですが、別の人が親指と人差し指でネジ穴から

5 落ちないように軽く支えてください。

6 各班からペットボトルを取りに来てください。

太陽電池組み立て終わったら、車輪をペットボトルの下に付けて、上に太陽電池をつけて

7 完成させてください。

8 ペットボトルを押させている人、つける人、分担作業で行いますよ。

9 出来上がりましたか。

10 では、みんなで校庭に出て、校庭で走らせてみましょう。

土の上はでこぼこしていて、走るのが難しいですから、コンクリートの上で走らせて

11 ください。

12 燃料は石油や石炭でなく、太陽の光だけなのです。

13 太陽の光だけで電気が使えるのはすごいですね。

電気を起こすには、太陽電池以外にも風の力を使った風力発電や身近なところだと

14 手動式で起こせる発電機もあります。

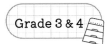
Grade 3 & 4

Let's make a solar car!

Teacher

1. As written in the Assembly Instructions ③, do not mistake the orientation of the gears.

2. And screw fastening mentioned in instruction manual ⑤.

This is probably the first time for you to use a screwdriver to fasten screws, if you have

3. done it before, please take the lead and turn it well.

If you don't put it in the screw hole and turn it with your finger a little, the screw will fall out of

4. the screw hole.

The screw is also small so when turning with a screwdriver, another person should

5. support it lightly with their thumb and forefinger so that it does not fall out of the screw hole.

6. Please come and get a plastic bottle for each group.

After the solar cell assembly is complete, attach the wheels to the bottom of the plastic bottle

7. and the solar cell to the top.

We will do this by dividing the work into two groups: those who push the PET bottle and

8. the person who attaches the wheels to the PET bottle.

9. Is it done?

10. Then we will all go out to the schoolyard.

Let them run in the schoolyard. It is difficult to run on dirt because it is bumpy, so let them

11. run on concrete.

12. The fuel is not oil or coal, only sunlight.

13. It is amazing that we can use only sunlight to generate electricity.

In addition to solar cells, there are other ways to generate electricity, such as wind power

generation using the power of the wind, and in more familiar places, generators that can be

14. operated manually.

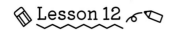

高学年

立体パズルを作ろう

先生

1 今日は1年生の歓迎会で行うゲーム用の立体パズルを作ります。

2 牛乳パック4個持ってきてくれていますね。

3 牛乳パックをサイコロ状の立方体にします。

4 4つの立方体で大きな立方体になることと、一つの立方体には6つの面があることを利用してパズルを作ります。

5 どんなパズルかというと、一つの絵が4つに分割してあって、各立方体に一枚ずつ張り付けて、立方体を回転させて、正しい絵を作るパズルです。

6 6つの面の絵柄をそれぞれ考えてください。

7 絵柄は自分で決めていいですが、あまりかけ離れた絵柄にはしないでください。

8 それぞれ、どんな絵柄にするか決めましたか。

9 では、絵柄を描く紙を配りますよ。

10 みんな紙は行き渡りましたか。

11 そしたら、まず、紙を2度折り曲げて広げてください。

12 その折り目のところで後で4つに分割します。

13 下書きは鉛筆でおこない、パスで塗ってください。

14 絵柄がよくわからないときは、後ろの本棚から図鑑を持ってきて見ながら描いてください。

Grade 5 & 6

Let's make a 3D puzzle!

Teacher

Today we are going to make a 3 D puzzle for a game we will play at the welcome party for

the first graders.

You have brought four milk cartons, right?

We will make the milk cartons into dice-shaped cubes.

We are going to make a puzzle based on the fact that four small cubes make a large cube,

and that a cube has six faces.

What kind of puzzle is this? Imagine having a picture on each side of the larger cube.

When you divide it into the smaller cubes, the picture becomes jumbled and you have

to rotate the smaller cubes to put the picture back together again.

Please think of a picture for each of the six sides.

You can decide the pattern yourself, but please do not make the patterns too different.

Have each of you decided what kind of design you would like to use?

Now, I will hand out the paper you will use to draw the patterns.

Has everyone been given a sheet of paper?

Okay, please fold the paper in half.

Then fold it in half again.

Please sketch your design with a pencil and then use a crayon to color it in.

If you are not sure of the pattern you want to use, bring an encyclopedia from the bookshelf

behind you and refer to it.

高学年

立体パズルを作ろう

先生

では、次に、牛乳パックで立方体を作りますよ。段ボールを持ってきました。

立方体はこんな段ボールのように作ります。

横面のりしろ部分の隙間に上の面のりしろ部分を差し込むようになっていますね。

これで、強度も高まるし、糊付けしなくてもふたが開かなくなりますね。

これから紙を1枚配りますから、牛乳パックの幅を調べて、

その寸法を元に切り体の寸法を、書き出してください。

皆さん、もう一回、先生の方を見てください。

段ボールの底は牛乳パックの底と同じですね。

段ボールの横面と前面と後面はどうですか。寸法が違いますよ。

よく見て、寸法を書き出してください。

牛乳パックは正四角柱です。

どの面が前面でも横面でも構いませんよ。

のりしろは、後面が3cm、横面が2cmとしましょう。

では、まず、各面の切り取る高さの部分に切取り線をサインペンで書いてください。

底面からの寸法を各面両端に印をつけて定規を当てて直線を引きますよ。

あらかじめ、のりしろの部分として曲げるところには点線で引いておくと後で作業が
しやすいです。

切取り線は引けましたか。

そしたら、カッターナイフで切り取りますよ。

カッターナイフを準備してください。

カッターナイフで切り取るときは、引いた線が
見えるところに定規を当てて、定規に沿って切りますよ。

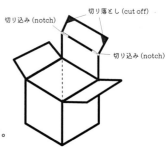
切り落とし (cut off)
切り込み (notch)
切り込み (notch)

定規線分が書いてない背中の部分をあてて、カッターナイフは45度の角度で、
一回で切り取ろうとせず、何回が当てて切り取りますよ。

定規を押さえている手が動かないとにしないと、何本も切取り線が出てしまいますよ。

面の寸法が違いますからね、その部分は折り目にカッターナイフを当てて不要な長さを
切り取ってください。

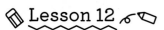

Grade 5 & 6

Let's make a 3D puzzle!

Teacher

1 Next, let's make a cube out of a milk carton. I have brought a cardboard box.

2 When you are finished, the cube should look like this cardboard box.

3 It is designed so that the top flap can be inserted into the gap at the side of the box.

4 This will make it stronger and prevent the lid from opening without gluing.

I will now hand out a sheet of paper, please check the width and the dimensions of your

5 milk carton and how you are going to cut it.

6 Everyone, please look at me one more time.

7 The bottom of the cardboard is the same as the bottom of the milk carton.

8 What about the side, front, and back of the cardboard? Each of the length is different.

9 Please check carefully and write down the measurements exactly.

10 A milk carton is a square prism.

11 It doesn't matter which side is the front or the side.

12 Let's say the glue allowance is 3 cm on the rear side and 2 cm on the side.

13 Now, first, use a non-permanent black marker to mark where you will be cutting.

Use a ruler to measure the dimensions from the bottom of each corner up to where you want

14 your line to be then connect the lines with a ruler.

It will be easier later if you draw a dotted line for the area you want to bend for the glue

15 allowance.

16 Has everyone drawn a line where you are going to cut?

17 Then, let's cut it out with a utility knife.

18 Please prepare your utility knife.

When cutting with a utility knife, place a ruler where

19 you can see the line you drew, and cut along the ruler.

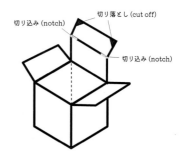

切り落とし (cut off)

切り込み (notch)

切り込み (notch)

You should place the knife along the opposite side of the ruler, where there are no measurements.

20 The utility knife should be angled at 45 degrees and don't try to cut everything out at once.

21 Also, If the hand holding the ruler is tight, you will end up with several cut lines.

Since the measurement of each side are different, you can just crop out whatever areas are

22 unnecessary.

立体パズルを作ろう

高学年

先生

1 はい、切取り終わりましたね。ちょっと先生の方を見て。

2 段ボールのふたの面の部分の折り目の部分を見てください。

3 まっすぐになっていませんね。

4 角が切り取ってあります。

5 同じように、今度ははさみを使って、切り取った牛乳パックののりしろ部分の角を切り取ってください。

6 折り曲げやすいようにのりしろの端を5㎜程切り込んでください。目測でいいですよ。

7 出来上がったら、のりしろ部分を折り曲げて、立方体の箱にしてみてください。

8 では、いよいよ牛乳パックの立方体に、さっき皆さんが作った絵柄を切り取って貼っていきますよ。

9 絵柄を貼るときは、紙用ボンドを使います。

10 ボンドを塗って貼りますが、その前にやっておくことがあります。

11 牛乳パックの表面はビニールのようなポリエチレン樹脂でコーティングしてありますと言いましたね。

12 これで表面がつるつるです。

13 そこで、表面のコーティングを紙やすりで軽く削り落としてください。

14 ボンドを塗りやすくするためだけなので、丁寧に磨く必要はありません。

15 どの面もまんべんなく紙やすりで磨いてコーティングを削ってください。

16 はい、そしたら、絵柄をはさみで切り取って、絵柄の裏にボンドを塗りましょう。

17 ボンドは少しの量でもすぐにくっつきます。へらで薄く面全体に塗ってください。

18 6枚の絵柄を順番に切り取って、糊付けして貼っていきますよ。

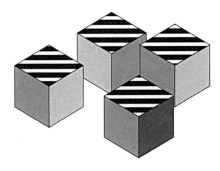

Let's make a 3D puzzle!

Grade 5 & 6

Teacher 📢

1. You have finished cutting out the pieces, right? Ok, please look at me for a bit.
2. Okay now, look at the folded part of the cardboard lid.
3. It is not straight.
4. The corners have been cut out.
5. In the same way, use scissors to cut off the corners of the cut-out milk carton.
6. Measuring it by eye, cut off about 5mm from the edge of the glue zone.
7. When you are done, fold the glue zones and turn it into a cube.
8. Now, it's time to cut out and paste the patterns you just made on the milk carton cube.
9. When attach the pictures, use glue.
10. Before applying the glue, there is something that needs to be done.
11. I said that the surface of the milk carton is coated with a polyethylene resin like vinyl.
12. This makes the surface smooth.
13. So, please remove the surface coating lightly with sandpaper.
14. It is not necessary to polish it too much because we only need to make it easier to apply the glue.
15. Please polish all surfaces evenly with sandpaper to scrape off the coating.
16. Yes, then cut out the pictures, with scissors and apply the craft glue to the back.
17. A small amount of glue is enough using a spatula to apply it thinly and evenly over the entire surface.
18. Cut out the 6 patterns one by one, add glue and then attach them.

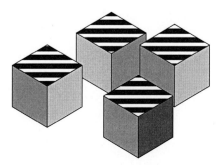

高学年

木版画を作ろう

先生

皆さんは、この絵を見たことがありますか。

棟方志功さんの作品です。

この作品は版画で作られています。

版画とは、木の板を彫刻刀で彫り、その板に墨を塗り、それを和紙に印刷した絵画です。

版画は必要性から生まれました。

版画を5年生になって説明を受けて、棟方志功先生の作品を見ると、とても難しそうに感じると思いますが、皆さんが幼稚園や小学校1年生に時に作った年賀状に押すイモに文字や絵を掘ったイモ版も、いろんなところにインクにつけて押している可愛いスタンプも原理は全く同じです。

彫刻刀や小刀で平面を掘って凸凹をつけて、インクをつけて押す。

使いすぎて凸凹が削れるまで何度でも同じ絵や文字を押し続けることができます。

版画という技術は中国から日本に伝わりました。1300年前ころには、仏教の経典やお釈迦様の姿を刷った版画が出てきています。

中国で発明された版画の技術はヨーロッパやイスラムにも伝えられ、それが進化して銅板を使った活版印刷になっていきます。

江戸時代初期に日本にも伝えられますが、漢字、ひらがら、カタカナという複雑な文字表記法やその後の長い鎖国政策の影響もあり、日本では活版印刷は普及せず、木版画技術が日本独特の技術として発達していきます。

墨一色だった木版画は、いろんな色を使ったカラー版画に進化しました。

木版画でこれだけの色とデザインを出せる技術は世界中を驚かせました。

明治時代にはたくさんの浮世絵が海外に流出しました。

なぜだと思いますか。

日本人にとってはあまりに身近すぎて、その価値と技術のすばらしさに気付かなかったからです。

この絵を知っていますか。
浮世絵と言います。

Let's make a woodblock print

Teacher

Have you ever seen this picture?

It is an artwork by Shiko Munakata.

This work is made of woodblock prints.

A woodblock print is a painting made by carving a wooden board with an engraving knife, applying ink to the board, and printing it on Japanese paper.

Printmaking was born out of necessity.

The principle is exactly the same as the potato prints you made in kindergarten and first grade of elementary school, which you used to stamp your New Year's cards, and the cute stamps you dip in ink and stamp in various places.

An engraver or small knife is used to dig a flat surface and make bumps, which are then dipped in ink and pressed on paper.

The same picture or character can continue to be stamped over and over again until it starts to wear out.

The technique of printmaking was introduced to Japan from China, and around 1,300 years ago, prints of Buddhist scriptures and images of Buddha appeared.

Printmaking technology invented in China was also introduced to Europe and Islam, where it evolved into letterpress printing using copper plates.

Although it was introduced to Japan in the early Edo period (1603-1867), due to the complicated writing system of kanji, hiragana, and katakana, and the long isolation policy that followed, letterpress printing did not spread in Japan, and woodblock printing technology developed as a uniquely Japanese technique.

Originally ukiyo-e was monochrome, but it evolved into color prints using various colors.

The technology that could produce so many colors and designs in woodblock prints surprised the world.

A lot of Ukiyo-e were lost overseas during the Meiji period.

Why do you think this was?

Because they were too familiar to Japanese people, and they did not appreciate its value and the excellence of the technique.

Do you know this picture?
It is called ukiyo-e.

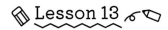

Lesson 13

高学年

木版画を作ろう

先生

1 日本で進化した独特の印刷手法である版画の基礎を学習するのが木版画工作です。

2 日本の伝統技術を学習します。

3 では、まず、木版画工作に使う彫刻刀の説明をします。

4 彫刻刀には、丸刀・三角刀・平刀・切り出し刀の四種類があります。

5 丸刀は、最も使いやすい彫刻刀で広い部分を彫り進むときに使います。

6 大小二種類の刀があり線の太さや彫る広さに合わせて使い分けます。

7 三角刀は細い線や鋭い線を彫ることができます。

8 平刀は、平らに削れ、丸刀などの彫り跡を削るときによく使います。

9 切り出し刀は、切り込みを入れるのに用いる刀で、細部を加工するときに使いやすく、平刀のように、広い面を削ることも出来ます。

10 次に使い方です。

11 丸刀・三角刀・平刀は、同じ使い方です。

12 主な持ち方は鉛筆を持つようににぎり、一方の親指をみねに当ててほります。

13 広い面をほるときは鉛筆のように持ち、一方の親指をえじりにおし当ててほります。

14 切り出し刀の使い方は他とは違います。

15 少し深ぼりをするときは、えをつつむように持ち、片方の指先をグリップに当ててほります。

16 えをつつむように持ち、かた方の指先をグリップに当ててほります。

17 線にそってほるときは鉛筆を持つようににぎり、親指をみねに当てておし切ります。

18 深ぼりをするときは先を手前に向けてにぎり、引き切ります。彫刻刀は刃物ですから、刃先の進行方向に手を置くと大変危険です。

19 このような左手の置き方はしないでください。

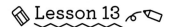

Grade 5 & 6

Let's make a woodblock print

Teacher

Learning the basics of woodblock printmaking, a unique printing technique that evolved in Japan, will help you to understand the basics of printmaking.

Let's learn these traditional Japanese techniques.

First, let me explain the engraving knives used in woodblock printmaking.

There are four types of engraving knives: round, triangular, flat, and cut out knives.

The round knife is the easiest to use and is used for carving large areas.

There are two types of round knives, large and small, and they should be used according to the thickness of the line and the size of the area to be engraved.

The triangular knives can be used to engrave thin or sharp lines.

The flat knives can be used to carve flat areas and are often used to flatten areas originally carved by other knives, such as the round knife.

The cut-out knives are used to cutting incisions into the surface. It is easy to use when carving details, and like the flat blade, it can also be used to carve large surfaces.

Next, let's take a look at how to use these knives.

The round, triangular, and flat knives are used in the same way.

The main way to hold the knife is to grip it like you would hold a pencil, and then place one thumb on the edge of the knife.

When carving a large surface, hold it like a pencil and press the thumb firmly against the edge.

The use of the cut-out knife is different from the others.

When you want to make a slightly deeper cut, hold the cutter as if you were squeezing the edge, and press the fingertips of the other hand against the grip.

To print along a line, grip the pencil as if you were holding a pencil, and press the thumb against the edge to cut.

When you want to do a deep cut, grip the knife with the tip facing forward and pull it backwards.

The sculpture knife is a knife, so it is very dangerous to place your hand in the direction in which the knife is moving.

Do not place your left hand like this.

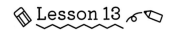
高学年

木版画を作ろう

先生

1 では、いよいよ木版画工作に入りましょう。

2 まずは下絵を描きます。

3 次に、下絵を版画用の板に上の部分をセロテープで止めて貼ってください。

4 下絵と板の間にカーボン紙を挟めます。

5 カーボン紙の表、つやのある方です、それが板の面ですよ。

6 挟みましたか。

7 そしたら、下絵の線を鉛筆の削っていない方の端でなぞってください。

8 十分に注意しながら、紙が破れない程度に強めになぞらないと板に線が付きませんよ。

9 出来ましたね。そしたら、ゆっくりと下絵をカーボン紙を外して下さい。

10 板の上に下絵の線が付いていますね。

11 では、マーカーで、その線の上をなぞってください。

12 ふと目になぞってくださいね。

13 線の部分を残して彫りますから、細いと彫っている途中に割れてしまったりしますよ。

14 では、彫刻刀で彫りますよ。

15 滑り止めシートの上に板を置いてください。

16 絶対に間違えてはいけないのは、黒い線は彫らないですよ。

17 その横を彫るんですよ。

18 良いですね。まず、三角刀で線の横をなぞって切っていってください。

19 板を横にしたり、さかさまにしたりして、切りやすくしてください。

20 そしたら、丸刀で、その切ったところを彫っていきます。

21 削りかすが板の上にあると彫る場所を間違えますよ。

22 時々板の上から取り除きます。

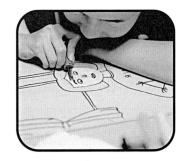

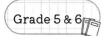

Grade 5 & 6

Let's make a woodblock print

Teacher

1. Now, let's start making a woodblock print.

2. First, draw a rough sketch.

3. Next, attach the rough sketch to the printmaking board by fastening the top part with cellophane tape.

4. Place a piece of carbon paper between the board and the rough sketch.

5. The front side of the carbon paper, the glossy side, should face the woodblock.

6. Have you placed it yet?

7. Then, trace your drawings with the unsharpened edge of a pencil.

8. Try to trace carefully without tearing the paper, otherwise the carbon will not appear on the woodblock.

9. You are done, right? Then, slowly remove the carbon paper from the draft sketch.

10. You can see the lines printed on the wooden board, right?

11. Now, take a marker and trace over the line.

12. Please trace boldly.

13. If your line is too thin, you may make a mistake during the process of carving.

14. Now, let's start the sculpture.

15. Place the board on the non-slip sheet.

16. Make sure not to make mistakes when carving the black line.

17. You have to sculpt around it.

18. Good. First, use a triangular knife to trace around where you will cut.

19. You can turn the board upside down or do anything you need to make it easier to sculpt.

20. Then, with the round knife, dig out the area where you made the cut.

21. If there are carving residue on the board, you will be confused about where to carve.

22. So, it is important to clean the board from time to time.

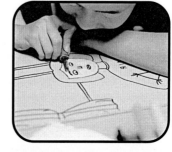

高学年

万年カレンダーを作ろう

先生

今日は、6年生を送る会で、6年生にプレゼントする万年カレンダーの制作をします。

では、万年カレンダーの基本の物を見てもらいますね。

これが万年カレンダーです。

4つのサイコロが入っています。

皆さんから見て一番左のサイコロは月が、次の二つのサイコロに日が、一番右のサイコロに曜日が書いてあります。

サイコロは面はいくつあるか分かりますね。

前の授業で立体パズルを作りましたからすぐにわかりますね。

そう、6面あります。

各サイコロの6面を使って毎日のカレンダーを表示します。

各サイコロの数字や曜日の書き方については後で説明します。

先ずは制作にかかりましょう。

今回使う材料は、A5サイズのベニア板2枚、20mm角の角材です。

道具は、のこぎり、糸鋸、錐、彫刻刀、金づち、釘、接着剤、アクリル絵の具、筆、紙やすり、工作用ニスです。

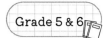
Grade 5 & 6

Let's make a perpetual calendar!

Teacher

1 Today, we are going to make a perpetual calendar as a graduation gift to the 6th graders at their send-off party.

2 Let me show you a typical perpetual calendar.

3 Here it is.

4 There are four dice inside.

5 The leftmost dice, as you see it, has the month, the next two dice have the date, and the rightmost dice has the day of the week.

6 You can see how many sides the dice have.

7 You can easily figure it out because we made a 3D puzzle in the previous lesson.

8 Yes, it has six sides.

9 The six sides of each dice are used to display a daily calendar.

10 I will explain how to write the numbers and days of the week on each dice later.

11 First, let's get to work.

12 The materials we will use this time are two A5 size veneer boards and a 20 mm squares.

13 Tools we will use are saw, hacksaw, cones, carving knife, hammer, nails, glue, acrylic paint, brushes, sandpaper, and varnish.

Lesson 14 　｜　図工　｜　Arts and Crafts

高学年

万年カレンダーを作ろう

先生

1. A5 の板を後ろの板にして、その前に万年カレンダーをつけます。

2. 下絵は寸法を適当すると、実際に板を切ったり、切り抜いたりするときに困ってしまいますから、スケッチブックに、後板の寸法の枠を作って、その中に定規やコンパスを

3. 使って長さを考えながら描いてください。

4. それができたら、実際にどんな色にするか、色鉛筆で塗って見てください。

5. 先に、今回使う工具について説明をします。

6. まず、万年カレンダー用に角材を切断して、サイコロを作ります。

　使うのは、のこぎりです。のこぎりは両方に刃がありますが、刃の目の大きさが違います。

7. 目の粗いが縦引き用、目の細かい方が横引き様です。

8. 縦引きとか横引きというのは、板を見てください。

9. 板には繊維が走っていますね。

10. この繊維に沿って切るのが縦引き、繊維を横断して切るのが横引きです。

11. 角材からサイコロを切り取るときは繊維を切断しますから、目の細かい横引きを使います。

12. 角材の面の寸法を測ってください。縦 20 ㎜、横 20 ㎜ですね。

13. いま、先生は 2 ㎝と言わず 20 ㎜と言いました。

　なかなか長さを㎜で使うことはないので慣れていないでしょうが、工作をするにあたっては寸法はできるだけ正確に表示しないと、曲がったり隙間ができたりしますから、

14. ㎝でなく、㎜で表示していきます。

15. 面の寸法が 20 ㎜×20 ㎜ですから、切り取る寸法も 20 ㎜ですね。

16. ですから、定規で角材の 4 面すべてに 20 ㎜の直線を引いてください。

　一面だけ、あるいは 2 面だけ寸法を引いて、あとの面は書かないで切り取っては絶対に

17. いけません。

18. 20 ㎜の幅で切り取れているか直線を確認しながら切っていきます。

19. 角材の切り取る面を机より前に突き出します。

20. 角材を左手でしっかり押さえて固定します。

　切り取る面の角、手前でも遠い方でもどちらでもよいですが、遠い方がやりやすいです。

21. 面に目の細かい方の歯を当てます。

　そしたら、ゆっくりと直線からずれないようにしながら、刃を斜めに入れながら

22. 切り出します。刃が切り口にはまったら、今度は細かく早く動かします。

23. 常に直線からどの切り口も外れていないか確認しながら、のこぎりを引きます。

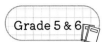

Lesson 14 · 図工 · Arts and Crafts

Grade 5 & 6 — Let's make a perpetual calendar!

Teacher

1. Put an A5 board as the back board with the perpetual calendar in front of it.

   If you don't measure the rough sketch properly, you will have trouble when you actually cut out
2. the board, so make a frame in your sketchbook with the dimensions of the back board.
3. Also use a ruler or compass to make your drawing.
4. Once that is done, think about what color you actually want to use and color with colored pencils.
5. Before I go any further, let me explain about the tools we will be using.
6. First, to use in the perpetual calendar, we will cut a square piece of wood and make a dice.

   We will use a saw to do this. The saw has blades on both sides, but the size of the blades are
7. different. The coarser blade is for vertical cutting and the finer blade is for horizontal cutting.
8. To determine whether a saw is for vertical or horizontal sawing, look at the board.
9. The board has fibers running through it.

   When cutting along the fibers we need a vertical cut, and when cutting across the fibers,
10. we need a horizontal cut.

    When cutting a dice from a square piece of lumber, we need to cut across the fibers,
11. so a horizontal using a finer blade should be used.
12. Measure the dimensions of the face of the square timber. It is 20 mm long and 20 mm wide.
13. I just said 20 mm, not 2 cm.

    Perhaps you are not used to hearing measurements in mm, however, in order to make crafts,

    dimensions must be indicated as accurately as possible, or else you will end up finding bends
14. or gaps.
15. Since the dimension of the surface is 20 mm x 20 mm, the dimension to be cut out is also 20 mm.
16. Therefore, use a ruler to draw a straight line of 20 mm on all four sides of the square timber.

    You should never cut out only one or two sides without drawing the dimensions of the other
17. sides.

18. Check the straight lines to make sure you are cutting at a 20 mm width.
19. The side of the square timber to be cut out should be pushed out in front of the desk.
20. Hold the square timber firmly in place with your left hand.

    Starting with the corner, position your body not too close nor too far away, though perhaps
21. a little far away is easier.

    Then, slowly cut out the material, inserting the blade at an angle, making sure not to deviate
22. from a straight line. Once the blade is in the cut, move the blade quickly and smoothly.

    Always check to make sure that none of the cuts deviate from a straight line while pulling
23. the saw.

高学年

万年カレンダーを作ろう

先生

1 のこぎりは刃物ですから、振り回したり、人に向けたりしてはいけませんよ。

それと、角材が動くと切取りが難しいですから、のこぎりを引くときは他の人が角材を
2 押さえるのを手伝ってください。

3 いいですか。

4 角材から一人4個ずつサイコロを切りとりますよ。

5 次に、サイコロを入れる箱を作ります。

6 箱はA5サイズのもう一枚の板から切り取ります。

7 これも同じように定規を当てて、直線で切り取ります。

8 切り取る板は底板と前板、それと側板2枚になります。

9 これで後ろ板のない箱を作って、後板に釘で打ち込んで固定します。

10 前板の横の長さは後板の横の長さと同じです。

11 前板の高さはサイコロが20mmですから同じ20mmします。

12 底板ですが、箱を見てください。

13 底板の側面に横板が、前面に前板がついていますね。

つまり、2枚の横板の厚みを加えた横の長さが後ろ板の横の長さと同じになりますから、
14 横板2枚の厚みを引いた長さになります。

15 横板の幅は底板の幅と同じ寸法、高さは前板と同じ寸法になります。

16 ベニア板を触って見てください。

17 つるつるした面とすこし目が粗い面があります。

18 つるつるした面が表です。

17 前板、横板は表面が外側になるように、底板は内側になるようにします。

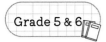
Let's make a perpetual calendar!

Grade 5 & 6

Teacher

1 We will do this in groups. Because the saw is sharp, don't play with it or point it at people.

Also, if the wood moves, it will be difficult to cut, so when you use the saw, please let another

2 person hold the wood from the other side.

3 Is that clear?

4 Each person will cut four dice from one piece of wood.

5 Next, we will make a box to put the dice in.

6 The box is cut from another A5 size board.

7 As we did before, use a ruler to cut a straight line.

8 We'll be cutting the front, the bottom, as well as the two sides.

After cutting, we are going to make a box without a back. The box will be attached to the back

9 board with screws to fix it in place.

10 The horizontal length of the front board is the same as that of the back board.

11 The height of the front board should be the same 20mm as the dice is 20mm.

12 As for the bottom board, please look at the box.

13 You can see the bottom piece, plus the two side pieces, add up in length to the back plate.

In other words, the horizontal length of the bottom board should be the same as that of the

14 back board minus the thickness of the two side boards.

For the side plates, the width of the side board is the same dimension as the width of

15 the bottom board, and the height is the same dimension as the front board.

16 Please touch the veneer board.

17 There is a smooth side and a slightly coarse side.

18 The smooth side is the front.

Make sure that the front and side panels face outwards and the front bottom panel should

19 be on the inside of the box.

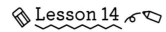
高学年

万年カレンダーを作ろう

 先生

万年カレンダーの仕組みついて理解しましょう。

立方体は 4 個あります。左の一つは月です。

真ん中の 2 つで日を、右の一つが曜日です。

まず、一番工夫を必要とする日について考えてみます。

カレンダーでは 1 日〜 31 日までの 31 通りの数字を表示させる必要がありますから、数字の配置方法について少し頭を使います。

まず、「1 日〜 10 日」までを表現するためには、それぞれに「0」の面が含まれる必要があります。

01、02、・・・10 は、0 を一つしか使っていないので、どちらかにあればよいように見えますが、0 が一つの立方体にしかない場合、その立方体に書いてある他の面の数字の日が使えません。

次に「11 日」と「22 日」の数字が連続する日付を示すためには、両方に「1」および「2」の面が含まれる必要があります。

0・1・2 をふたつの立方体に書き入れるのは必然として、残った 3 〜 9 までの数字をそれぞれの立方体に割り振ります。具体的には下記のとおりです。

一つ目（0・1・2・3・4・5）　二つ目（0・1・2・6・7・8）

9 が足りなくなりますが、9 は 6 をひっくり返すと使えます。

これで、日付けの割り振りはわかりましたね。

次に、月ですが、6 面ありますね。

月は 12 か月ですから、6 面の半分ずつにして割り振ると使えます。

同様に曜日は 7 つですが、7 曜日あり、立方体は 6 面ですからどれかの 2 つの曜日を一つの面に書くことになりますが、週末は楽しい曜日ですから間違えることはほぼありませんから、土曜日と日曜日を一つの面を半分にして記載します。

これで万年カレンダーが出来上がります。

図工

Arts and Crafts

Grade 5 & 6

Let's make a perpetual calendar!

Teacher
📢

1 Let's try to understand how a perpetual calendar works.

2 There are four cubes. The left one is the month.

3 The two in the middle are for the date, and the one on the right is the week.

4 First, let's consider the middle ones, the date, as they require the most creativity.

Since the calendar needs to display 31 different numbers from the 1st to the 31st, we have to

5 be a little clever about how to arrange the numbers.

6 First, in order to represent the "1st ~ 10th," each cube must contain a "0" side.

Since 01, 02, ... 10 uses only one 0, you might think we only need to write one 0, but if the 0 is

only on one cube, the days of the numbers on the other sides written on that cube cannot be

7 used.

Next, in order for the numbers "11" and "22" to indicate consecutive dates, both cubes must

8 contain a "1" and a "2" side.

Seeing that we need to write 0, 1, and 2 on the two cubes, and the remaining numbers

9 from 3 to 9 are assigned to each cube we would allocate the numbers as follows.

10 First cube (0, 1, 2, 3, 4, 5) Second cube (0, 1, 2, 6, 7, 8)

11 The 9 will be missing, but 9 can be used by turning the 6 blocks over.

12 Now you know how to assign the date.

13 Next, we have the month, there are 6 sides, right?

14 There are 12 months, so we can use half of each of the 6 sides to divide the month.

Similarly, there are seven days of the week, but since there are seven days of the week and

the cube has six sides, you have to write any two days of the week on the same side.

Since the weekend is fun and it is almost impossible to make a mistake with it, we will list

15 Saturday and Sunday as one half of one side.

16 This makes a perpetual calendar.

日曜大工とDIY

休みの日に棚を作ったり犬小屋を作る木工的な作業を趣味でやることを日本では、日曜大工といいます。最近は、日曜大工と言わず、DIY という言葉が使われるようになってきました。

DIY は、Do-It-Yourself を略したもので、自分で物を作る意味で、第二次世界大戦で、廃墟になったロンドンを元軍人たちが「Do-It-Yourself なんでも自分でやろう」を合言葉に、町の再建に取り組んだことが始まりです。「自分でやろう」の合言葉が、Do it "myself" でなく、"yourself" なのは、you は、一般的に人はだれでもいう意味を表すときに使われるからです。授業中に先生が生徒に "What happens if you boil the water?" と尋ねた場合の生徒の答えは "I" でなく、"you" で答えます。日本語でも、相手に「自分でやりなさい」という「自分」という人称、「自分でやります」という人称が違うのに、同一代名詞の使い方があります。

ちなみに、DIY と日曜大工は、少し違います。
日曜大工とは「休日にプロではない方が趣味で大工仕事を行うことをいい、主に木工作業のことをいいます。DIY でも木工で棚やテーブルを作ったりしますが、DIY は他にも雑貨やメイク用品などという、木工を使用しないでインテリアやファッション用品を作る時にも該当します。
つまりは木工作業を趣味で行うことを「日曜大工」、自身で木工作業を含めた手作り作業をすることを広く含んでいるのが「DIY」です。日本に DIY が入ってきたのは 1970 年代初頭で、やがて今のホームセンターとしてのスタイルが確立されていきました。

DIY する人	→ DIYer
日曜大工	→ home carpentry
糊付けする	→ to join things together using glue (接着剤であれば adhesive)
ガムテープ	→ adhesive tape もしくは packing tape
ガムテープをはがす	→ remove the packing tape
釘	→ nail,
釘を板に打ち付けるは	→ hit the nail でなく、nail a board で動詞の nail を使用。

体育
subject 6

P.E.

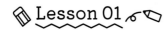
低学年

体育の基本

先生

1 体育の時間ですので、体操着に着替えます。

2 男子は、教室で着替えます。女子は、更衣室で着替えます。

着替えたら、男子は、脱いだ服は畳んで、イスの上に置いてください。

3 机の上には置かないでくださいね。

4 女子は、更衣室の棚に置いて下さい。

5 終わったら、運動場に集まってください。

6 では、整列してください。整列したら、まず、「気を付け」をします。

「気を付け」というのは、ちょっと、先生を見てください。このように、足をつけて、

つま先を開きます。背中をピンと伸ばして、腕も手の指先も、まっすぐにして、

7 体にピタッとつけます。

「前へ・・・ならえ。」と、先生が、号令をかけますから、両手を肩の高さまで上げて、

まっすぐ伸ばして、前の人に当たらないようにします。

8 「なおれ」と、先生が号令したら、手を下して体にピタッとつけます。

7 いいですね、「気を付け」のままだとつかれますね。

10 休めの号令をしたら、このような姿勢になってください。

左足を少し横に出して、両腕を後ろに回して、腰のあたりで手を組んでいます。

11 これが休めの姿勢です。

12 では、練習しますよ。「気をつけ！」「前へ・・・ならえ」「なおれ！」「休め！」

13 次に、座り方をやりますよ。

14 はい、先生の方を見てください。

このように背筋を伸ばし、腰を下ろして、両ひざを軽く曲げて、

15 手を、膝の少し下で組んで下さい。

16 「腰を・・・おろして」と先生が号令をかけたら、こうして座ってください。

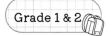

Lesson 01

The Basics of P.E.

Grade 1 & 2

Teacher

1 It is our first P.E. class, so we need to get changed first.

2 Boys will get changed in the classroom, and girls will go to the changing room.

3 Once you are dressed and ready, boys, please put your clothes on your chair, not on the desk.

4 Girls, you can put them on the shelf in the changing room.

5 After that, we will all line up on the school field.

6 Line up! Now, once we line up, I want you to stand up straight.

  This means, well, look at me; my feet are closed with my toes facing slightly outwards while

7 my arms and back are as straight as a pencil.

  When I say, "Face forward!", I want you to hold your hands up to the height of your shoulder,

  and stretch them to make sure they don't touch the person in front of you. Once I say,

8 "Fixed position!" I want you to put your hands back to your normal position.

9 Listen, I know that if you keep the fixed position all the time, you might get tired.

10 So when I say "Relax!" I want you to be like this.

11 Make a small step to your left, and clasp your hands together behind your back.

12 Let's practice: Stand still! Face forward! Fixed position!

13 Next, I am going to show you how to sit in a P.E. class.

14 Attention here, please.

  I want you to sit with your back straight, knees slightly bent and your hands holding your

15 legs in front of you.

16 When I say, "Sit down," this is the position that I want you to be in.

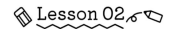

体育

P.E.

準備体操

低学年

先生

運動をする前に、けがをしないために、肩やひじ、背中やひざ、手首、足首などの準備運動をしなければいけません。

これをしないで、いきなり全速力で走ったり、ぶら下がったり、ボールけりをすると、ケガの元になります。

はい、全員立って、準備体操を始めますよ。

はい、「前へ ・・・ならえ」、両手を肩の高さで左右に広げて、隣の人とぶつからないように広がって。

では、足を少し広げて、背中をぴんと伸ばして、腕を大きく回します。

外回し、うち回し。1,2,3,4,2,2,3,4。

足をもっと開いて、体を前に丸めて、手は、足の指先に向けて、まっすぐ伸ばして、1,2,3,4、

はい、体を起こして、体を後ろにそらして、腕もまっすぐしたまま、後ろにそらして 5,6,7,8。

足を閉じて、左足を後ろに引いて、右膝をまげて、右膝の上に両手をおいて、

左足をのばして、1,2,3,4。足首を伸ばしてくださいね。

アキレス腱といって、大切なところをしっかり伸ばしますよ

両足揃えて、ジャンプしますよ、1,2,3,4。

足を少し開いて、右腕を、まっすぐ上に伸ばして、右の耳にあてて ・・・そのまま、体を左側に倒します 1.2.3.4。

体をもとに戻して、今度は、左腕を上に伸ばして、

左耳にあてて ・・・体を右側に倒します 1.2.3.4。

Grade 1 & 2

Warming up

Teacher

Before doing any sports, we need to do warm up exercises for our shoulders, elbows, back, knees, wrists and ankles, to avoid injuries.

If we skip warming up, and you run at full speed, hang from the bars or kick a ball, you could get injured.

Ok everyone. Stand up and get ready for warm up exercises.

Face forward! Stretch out your arms at shoulder level and make sure you don't hit the person next to you.

Stand with your feet wide, stretch your back and make big spinning movements with your arms.

Spin forward and backwards. 1,2,3,4,2,2,3,4.

Open your feet wider, roll your body forward, hands straight out, towards your toes, 1,2,3,4.

Go back to the original position then bend your body backwards, arms also straight, 5, 6, 7, 8.

Close your feet. Pull your left foot back, bend your right knee, put your hands on your right thigh, stretch out your left leg,1,2,3,4. Please extend your ankle.

This stretches the Achilles tendon, which is a very important part of the ankle.

Put both feet together and jump, 1,2,3,4.

Open your feet to your shoulders, stretch up your right arm touching your ear, then you bend your body to the left 1,2,3,4.

Back to your position, then stretch your left arm touching your left ear this time then bend your body to the right 1,2,3,4.

低学年 🎒

リズム遊び

先生 📣

1 今日から、音楽を聴きながら、リズムあそびをやりましょう。

2 音楽を聴いて、音楽に合わせてリズムを取ります。

3 まず、ステップの練習をして、ステップが出来るようになったら、体や腕を付けていきます。

4 はい、その場で足を挙げて、ステップを始めます。先生の手拍子に合わせて、

5 パン、パン、パン、パン、はい、1,2,3,4、1,2,3,4、

はい、右足を前に出して膝を曲げて、右足戻して、その場でステップ、1,2,3,4、

6 左足前に出して膝を曲げて、左足戻して、その場でステップします。

7 ステップのときに、腕を合わせて。

8 腕を大きく振って、ステップ。

手は腰に当てて、右足を前。かかとを付けて、つま先を立てて膝を伸ばして、戻す。

9 その場で一回ステップ。

左足も同じように、かかとを付けて、つま先を立てて膝を伸ばして、戻す。

10 その場で一回ステップします。

┌─── プラスワン　リズムの関連する単語 ───┐

pitch	ピッチ
rhythm	リズム
beat	ビート
tap on floor	床の上を軽くたたく
snap fingers	指を鳴らす
mirror a movement	動作をまねる

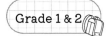

Lesson 03

Grade 1 & 2

Rhythm Play

Teacher

1. Today, we are going to exercise while listening to some music.

2. Listen to the music and let's exercise along with the rhythm!

3. First, we will practice the steps. Once we get the steps down, then we'll learn to move our body and arms along.

4. OK, please lift your feet and start stepping where you are.

5. Follow as I clap. (clap, clap, clap) 1, 2, 3, 4, 1, 2, 3, 4.

6. Put you right foot forward, bend your knee, put your right foot back and step there, 1-2-3-4, put your left foot forward, bend your knee, put your left foot back and step there.

7. Now, swing your arms with your steps.

8. Swing big and step.

9. Put your hands on your waist, put your right foot forward, touch your heel to the floor with your toes up. Stretch your knees, then go back to the same position and step once.

10. Do the same for your left foot. Put your left foot forward, touch your heel to the floor with your toes up, stretch your knees, then back to the same position and step once.

中学年

バランス遊び

先生

1 皆さん、両手を広げて、隣と当たらないように広がってください。

2 両手は広げたままですよ。

3 はい、左足を後ろに曲げて右足一本立ち！

4 はい、左足戻して。

5 ふらふらしてしまいますね。

6 これをバランスと言います。

7 サーカスで、一本のロープの上を歩いて渡る曲芸見たことがありませんか。

8 体のバランスが取れるとあんな曲芸もできます。

9 体のバランスがよくなるためには、体全体の動きが必要になります。

10 今日は、バランスをとれるようになるための運動をしてみましょう。

11 はい、まず、バランスボールに座ってみます。見ていてください。

12 頂点にまっすぐ座って、膝と腰の角度は直角にして。

13 では、先頭の人座ってみましょう。１０秒です。

14 後ろの人は、近くに行って、落ちないように支えてあげられる体制をとってください。

15 はい、後ろの人にボールを回して。どんどんやっていきますよ。

16 次は、バランスボールの上で腰を回しましょう。

17 頭は振れないようにして。

18 次は、バランスボールの上で、お尻を浮かせて弾んでみてください。

19 腕を振って足踏みをしましょう。

20 ボンボン、グルグル、ドンドン。

21 はい、バランスボールにもたれかかり、背筋を伸ばして上体そらしです。

22 両足の足の裏を床に吸い付かせて、お腹と背中に力をいれて。

23 体の左右のバランスをとらないと、どちらかに転がりますよ。

24 最後は、お腹と胸でバランスボールにかぶさって、左腕で腕立ての姿勢。

25 右腕はまっすぐ前に出して。はい、右腕で腕立て姿勢。左腕を前。

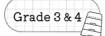

Lesson 04

体育

P.E.

Grade 3 & 4

Balance Activities

Teacher

1. Please spread out your hands so that they do not touch the next person.
2. Keep your hands outstretched.
3. Bend your left leg behind you and stand on your right leg only.
4. Ok, now put your left foot back down.
5. You felt really unsteady, right?
6. This is called Balance.

7. Have you ever seen a circus acrobat walk across a single rope?
8. If you can balance your body, you can do that kind of acrobatics.
9. The entire body needs to be in better balance.

10. Today, let's do some exercises to help you learn to balance.
11. First, sit on the balance ball. Please look at me.
12. Sit straight at the top, knees and hips at right angles.
13. Now, let's start with the person in the front row -please try to sit down for 10 seconds.
14. The next person in line should go close and stand by to support your classmate so that they do not fall.
15. Alright, pass the ball to the person behind you. We will keep practicing it.
16. Next, rotate your hips on the balance ball.
17. Do not swing your head.

18. Next, try bouncing on the balance ball with your hips.
19. Swing your arms and stomp your feet.
20. Bounce, bounce, round and round.

21. Ok, now lean on the balance ball, stretch your back, and keep your upper body straight.
22. Place both feet on the floor, and then put tension on the muscles in your stomach and back.
23. If you don't balance the left and right sides of your body, you'll roll over one way or the other.

24. Finally, cover the balance ball with your stomach and chest and get into a push-up position with your left arm.
25. Your right arm should be straight out in front of you. Now change positions, get into a push-up posture with your right arm and your left arm straight forward.

P.E.

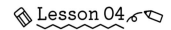

体育

P.E.

中学年

バランス遊び

先生

1. 用具係さん、用具室から人数分のフラフープを持ってきてください。
2. 大きさはバラバラで構いません。
3. 持ってくるときは、小さい輪は肩にかけて、大きな輪は二人で運んできてください。

4. フラフープって、知っていますね。腰で回して遊びます。
5. 腰に当てて、両手で地面と平行に持ち上げて支えます。
6. それから、腰と腕でフラフープを回転させる準備をして、ハイ！
7. どれだけ長くフラフープを落とさないで、腰に回り続けられるかがポイントです。

8. 世界大会もあり、何時間も回せる達人もいます。
9. フラフープを使って、色んな運動をします。

10. まず、全員、4列で並んでください。
11. フラフープは左手に立ててもってください。
12. 向こうの壁までフラフープを転がして壁にタッチして、まだ転がして戻ってきてください
13. フラフープを転がすときは、進行方法にまっすぐ立てて、上の部分を掴んで、前に回転させます。
14. バランスよく回転できれば長く転がりますが、力の入れ方が変だとすぐに倒れてしまいます。

15. 今日、初めての人もいると思います。
16. 最初は、うまく転がらないで倒れます。
17. 何度かチャレンジして、勘を掴んでください。
18. ハイ、先頭の人、準備してください。よーい、ピッ！

Balance Activities

Teacher

1. Okay, sports prefects please bring enough hula hoops from the equipment room.

2. Any size is fine.

3. When you bring them, carry the small ones on your shoulder and the large ones should be carried by two people.

4. You know what a hula hoop is, right? You play with it by spinning it around your waist.

5. Place it on your waist and lift and support it parallel to the ground with both hands.

6. Then get ready to spin the hula hoop with your hips and arms, ready? good!

7. The key is how long you can keep the hula hoop spinning around your waist without dropping it.

8. There are world competitions, and some masters can spin for many hours.

9. We use hula hoops for a variety of exercises.

10. First, everyone please line up in four rows.

11. Hold the hula hoop upright in your left hand.

12. I want you to roll the hula hoop to the other wall, touch the wall, and roll it back yet again.

13. To roll the hula hoop, stand it upright in the direction you want it to go, grasp the top, and rotate it forward.

14. If it can rotate in a balanced manner, it will roll for a long time, but if the force is applied in an odd manner, it will fall over quickly.

15. I think some of you are new to this today.

16. At first, it may not roll well and fall over.

17. Try a few times and try to get the feeling.

18. Alright, first people in the line, get ready. beep!

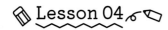

体育

P.E.

中学年

バランス遊び

先生

1 次に、2人ずつ組んで行います。

2 コートいっぱいに広がって、向かい合ってください。

3 はい、では、一人がフープを空中に投げて、もう一人はフープの中に入ります。

4 投げるときは、相手が入りやすいように、両手で持って、輪投げをする要領で、斜め上に、ちょうど二人の真ん中あたりが山なりのてっぺんに来るようなイメージで投げます。

5 入る方は、フープの動きを目で追いながら、フープの落ちてくる場所に移動します。」

6 出来るようになったら、二人の間の距離を少しずつ広げていって。

7 はい、次の運動です。

8 向かい合って、一人はコートの外のライン、一人はコートの真ん中のラインで向かい合ってください。

9 はい、それぞれ自分のフープをもって、同時に相手に転がしてください。

10 二人ともキャッチ出来たら、合格です。その場に座ってください。

11 はい、それでは、立ってください。

12 今度は投げてキャッチを行いますよ。

13 同時に相手に投げて、二人ともキャッチ出来たら、すごしずつ、距離を広げて下さい。

Grade 3 & 4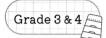

Balance Activities

Teacher

1 Next, we will play the game in pairs.

2 Spread out across the entire court and face each other.

Yes, now, one person will throw the hoop in the air and the other person will try to dive inside

3 the hoop.

When you throw the hoop, hold it with both hands so that the other person can easily enter,

4 and throw it diagonally upward, just as in a ring toss,

The person entering the hoop should move to the place where the hoop falls, while following

5 the movement of the hoop with your eyes.

6 Once you can do it, you can gradually increase the distance between the two of you.

7 Alright, so let's do the next exercise.

Face each other, one should stand on the outside line of the court and one on the middle line of

8 the court.

9 Now, each of you should hold your own hoop and roll it to your partner at the same time.

10 If you both catch it, you pass and please sit on the spot.

11 Ok, now please stand up.

12 Now we will do the throw and catch.

Throw the hula hoop to your partner at the same time, and if you both catch it, increase

13 the distance, little by little.

低学年

機械運動
鉄棒

先生

1 はい、皆さん、整列。前に・・・ならへ。なおれ。

2 今日は、鉄棒の練習をやりましょう。

3 良いですか、鉄棒を、肩の幅よりすこし広めに、両手でつかみます。

4 このように掴むときは、親指と他の指で、しっかりと挟んで掴みます。

5 掴んだら、腕に力を入れて、足で、地面をけって、上に飛び上がります。

6 体を前ななめにして、鉄棒にお腹が触れてかぶさります。

7 そしたら、あごを引いて、背中をのばしたままで、くるっと、まわります。

8 絶対に、手を離してはだめですよ。

9 くるっとまわったら、足を地面につけます。

10 これが前回りですね。練習しましょう。

11 体は、背を伸ばして、少し斜め前にしてください。

12 腕に力を入れる時とジャンプは、一緒にします。

13 そう、そう、飛びついて、上で止まって、ゆっくりと回転して着地しますよ。

では、先頭の人から始めますよ。鉄棒を両手で掴んでぶら下がって、体を前後に

14 振ってください。

15 足が地面に着かないようにして、体を振ってください。はい、後ろまで振ってください。

16 はい、そしたら、腕の間から足を入れて、両足を鉄棒に引っかかってください。

17 しっかり、足をまげて、足でぶら下がってください。

18 はい、足でぶら下がったら、体を振ってみてください。

19 はい、両手をもう一度鉄棒にかけて、両手で体を支えて、足を外して、床につけてください。

20 次の列の人、同じようにやってください。

先生

1 では、次に、後ろ向きから、足を鉄棒にかけましょう。

2 手の握り方を見てください。

3 先ほどとは、持ち方が違うのがわかるでしょ。

4 そして、背中を丸めて、足を、鉄棒の外から鉄棒に掛けます。

5 鉄棒に、足をしっかりと掛けたら、手を放して、はい、体が鉄棒にぶら下がります。

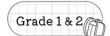
体育

P.E.

Gymnastics

Horizontal bar

Teacher

1. OK, everyone, "Face forward, line up!" "Fixed position".

2. Let's practice the horizontal bar today.

3. OK, so you grab the bar with both hands spaced at shoulder length.

4. When you grab the bar, make sure you use your thumb and the rest of your fingers to hold the bar tightly, like this.

5. Once you grab it tightly, put your strength in your arms and then kick off the ground and bring your body upwards using your legs.

6. As you rest on to the bar, your stomach should be touching and covering the bar.

7. Now, pull your chin in and flip forward, keeping your back straight.

8. Don't release your hands.

9. Once you successfully flip over, then land.

10. This is the forward turn. Let's take turns practicing.

11. You should keep your back stretched leaning slightly forward.

12. Use your arm strength and jump at the same time.

13. That's it, just like that, you jump on the bar, stop at the top, then slowly flip over and land.

14. Alright, starting from the person in front, please hang on to the bar and swing your body back and forth.

15. Swing your body so your feet don't touch the ground. Yes, swing as far back as you can.

16. And now, put your legs between your arms and hook yourself on the bar with both legs.

17. Bend your legs tightly and hang your body upside-down on the bar.

18. After you hang upside-down, try to swing.

19. Alright then, grab the bar again with your hands bending your body, then take your legs off the bar and stand on the ground.

20. The next person in the row please do the same.

Teacher

1. Now, let's do it backwards.

2. Watch how I grip the bar.

3. You can see it's a little different from before.

4. Roll your back and hook your legs from outside the bar.

5. After you hook your legs tightly on the bar, let go of your grip, now your body is hanging on the bar.

P.E.

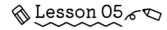
体育

P.E.

中学年

機械運動

鉄棒

先生

1 今日は、足掛け上がりと足掛け前まわりを練習しましょう。

　足掛け上がりは、両手で鉄棒をもって、ぶら下がり、体を丸めて、右足を両手の間からぬいて

鉄棒にかけて、左足をバーの真下より後ろまで振って、その勢いで、両腕で鉄棒の上に体を

2 もっていきます。

　一回でできない時は、ブランブランと振り子みたいにして、一二の三で、左足を後ろに

3 勢いよく持って行ってすばやく両腕で体を引き起こします。

4 鉄棒にかけているひざの裏がいたい人は教えてください。

5 鉄棒にタオルを巻きます。

6 はい、これが出来たら、足掛け前まわりを練習します。

7 足掛け上がりで、鉄棒の上に体があります。

　伸ばした足をしっかりと前後に振って勢いをつけ、その足を後ろに振って、

8 前周りをして一回転します。

9 背中と伸ばしている足はまっすぐ伸ばしてください。

10 足と背中が曲がると、回転が弱くなり、途中で止まってしまいます。

11 では、足掛け後ろまわりを練習しましょう。

12 要領は足掛け前まわりと同じです。

13 前に回るか、後ろに回るかの違いです。

　背中と伸ばした足をしっかり伸ばして、勢いをつけて、遠くを蹴るイメージで振り出して

14 回転します。

　膝の裏が鉄棒から離れないようにして、振りぬいた足は、鉄棒からくるっと後ろまで

15 回るようにします。

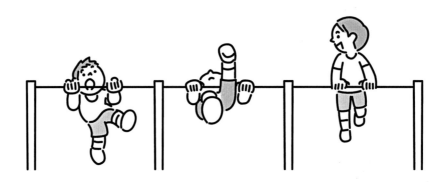

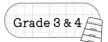

Lesson 05

Gymnastics

Horizontal bar

Teacher

1 Today let's practice knee swings on the bar.

In the knee swing, you hold the bars with both hands, and hang down. Then, roll your body, put your right foot between your hands on the bars, swing your left foot to the back of the bars,

2 and use the momentum of the swing to lift your body over the bars with both arms.

If you can't do it the first time, do it like a swinging pendulum. On the one, two, three, bring your

3 left foot strongly behind you and quickly bring your body up with both arms.

4 Please let me know if the backs of your knees start hurting while you are hanging on the bar.

5 In that case, I can wrap a towel around the bars.

6 Yes, once this is done, practice front knee swings.

7 Now your body is on the bars after doing the knee swings, right?

Now, swing the outstretched leg quickly back and forth to gain momentum, then swing that

8 leg backward and make a full rotation around the front.

9 Your back and outstretched legs should be straight.

10 If the legs and back are bent, the rotation is weaker and you will stop in the middle.

11 Now, let's practice the back knee swing.

12 It is basically the same as the front knee swing.

13 The difference is whether you turn forward or backward.

With your back and outstretched legs quickly extended, swing out and rotate with momentum

14 with the image of kicking far away.

The back of the knee should not leave the bars, and the swinging leg should turn around from

15 the bars to the back.

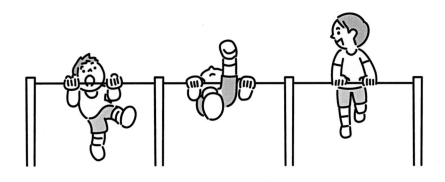

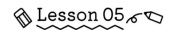

体育

P.E.

高学年

機械運動
鉄棒

先生

1. では、今日は、鉄棒の連続技を練習しましょう。

2. 逆上がり、膝掛け前回りはできるようになりましたね。

3. では、順番に連続してやってみましょう。

4. はい、4列になってください。

5. 最初の列の人は鉄棒につかまって逆上がりをします。

6. そしてそのまま右足を鉄棒に乗せて、踏み越しおりをやってください。

7. 右足を鉄棒の上にのせたら、左足を鉄棒の上を越しながら、右手を外して飛び降ります。

8. はい、次の列の人は逆上がりをして、鉄棒の上に乗ったら、そのまま足を後ろに振り上げて、空中で逆上がりをしますよ。

9. 足を振り上げていたら、あとは普通の逆上がりの要領です。

10. はい、次の列の人は、膝かけ上がりから、左足を鉄棒の上から抜いて、前下りします。

11. はい、全員ぶら下がって、左足を腕の間から抜いて、鉄棒に左足の膝を掛けて、勢いをつけて、鉄棒の上にあがりますよ。

12. はい、あがったら、ここで止まって、左足を鉄棒の上から抜くのに合わせて、右足に重心を掛けて飛び降ります。

13. はい、次の列に代わってください。

14. 今度は、ひざ掛け上がりから後方片膝かけ回転をやってみましょう。

15. はい、膝を掛けて、反対の足を思いっきり振って、鉄棒の上で止まります。

16. はい、そしたら、そのまま前方一回転して鉄棒の上で止まりますよ。

17. はい、そしたら、ひざ掛けしていない足を鉄棒の上から抜いて飛び降りてください。

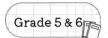

Gymnastics
Horizontal bar

Teacher

1 Today, let's continue to practice on the horizontal bar

2 You are now able to hang upside down and to circle the bar with your knees.

3 Now, let's do them in sequence and in order.

4 Let's get into lines of four.

5 The first person, please hold onto the horizontal bar and do a back hip circle.

6 Then without coming down, bring your right leg over the bar.

7 Once your right foot is on the bar, jump down with your left leg over the bar while removing your right hand.

8 The next students in line do a back hip circle, and once you are on the horizontal bar, swing your legs backwards and then do another back hip circle as you are in the air.

9 Once you swing your legs up, it is the same as for a regular back hip circle.

10 OK, the next student after that, go up from a kneeling position, pull your left leg off the top of the bar, and go down in front of them.

11 Okay everyone, please hang on to the bar. Pull your left leg out from between your arms, hang your left knee on the bar, and climb up to the top of the bar with a lot of momentum.

12 After climbing up, stop there. While you take your left leg from the top of the bar, incline towards the right and then jump off.

13 Good, please move on to the next row.

14 Now let's try a backward one-knee rotation from a kneeling position

15 Hang one knee on the bar and then swing the opposite leg as hard as you can. Stop at the top of the bar.

16 Yes, now make one front hip circle and stop again at the top of the bars.

17 OK, now jump off the bar with the leg that is not hooked.

低学年

水泳・水遊び

先生

1. 夏に一番楽しい遊びといえば、水泳ですね。

2. 小学校になると、プールがありますから、授業で水泳を楽しめます。

3. まずは、水着に着替えましょう。

4. 皆さん、水着とバスタオルと水泳帽を持ってきましたね。すべてに、名前が書いてありますね。確認してください。

5. では、女子は、先生と一緒に更衣室に行きます。

6. 男子は、教室で着替えます。

7. 着替えたら、バスタオルと水泳帽を持って、プールサイドに集合します。

8. プールサイドは、ぬれていますので、はだしで行きます。

9. 滑りますから、気を付けて、ゆっくり歩いてください。

10. 今日、プールに入らずに見学の人は、見学カードとボードを持って、一緒に並んで行って、見学者席で見学します。

11. はい、皆さん、バスタオルをタオル掛けに掛けてください。

12. 水泳帽をかぶってください。

13. では、プールに入る前に、準備体操をします。

14. 一列になって、プールサイドの周りを歩きます。ピッピッ。止まれ！

15. 先生の方に、体ごと向けて気を付け！

16. 準備体操をするとき、特にジャンプをしたりするときは、床がとても滑りやすいですから、気をつけてください。

17. 準備体操が終わったら、先生の前に整列！整列したら4列になってシャワーを浴びます。

18. 頭から足まで、身体全体浴びてください。

19. みんな、浴び終わりましたね。そしたら、いよいよプールに入ります。

Grade 1 & 2

Swimming

Teacher

1 | One of the best things to do during summer is swimming, right?

2 | In elementary school, we have a swimming pool so we can enjoy swimming lessons.

3 | We need to get changed first.

4 | Did you all bring a swimming suit, a bath towel, and a swimming cap? Your names are written on everything, right?

5 | Now, girls come with me to the changing room.

6 | Boys, please change in the classroom.

7 | After you get changed, take your towel and swimming cap and gather at the pool side.

8 | It's wet at the pool side so come barefooted.

9 | Be careful, it's slippery so walk slowly.

10 | If you are not going into the pool today and are just watching today, bring your observation card and board and line up with us and then sit in the observation seats.

11 | Everyone, please hang your towels here.

12 | Put on your swimming cap.

13 | Now we are going to warm up before we go in to the pool.

14 | Make a line and walk around the pool side. (whistle). Stop!

15 | Face me, stand up straight!

16 | Be careful not to slip when you do the warm up especially when you jump. The floor is very slippery.

17 | After warming up, walk back to me here and line up in 4 lines and get in the shower.

18 | Please wash yourself in the shower from your head all the way down to your feet.

19 | Now that everyone has finished taking a shower. We can go into the pool.

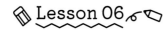 Lesson 06

低学年 　　　　　　　水泳・水遊び　　　　　 1

先生 📢

1. 全員、プールに入りましたね。では、まず、水に顔を浸けてみましょう。

2. 目をあけたまま水に浸けますよ。息を止めます。

3. 手を上に万歳して、はい、そのまま、腕をまっすぐ水の方に下ろしていき、それに合わせて、体を曲げて、顔を浸けます。

4. 顔を浸す間、息を止めてください。

5. 顔を浸けたら、10数えて、顔を上げます。1,2,3,4,…10。

6. はい、顔を上げてください。

7. 目を開けたまま水面に近づくと、怖いと感じると思うから、顔を浸けてしまってから、目を開いてみてください。

8. では、隣同士で向かい合ってください。

9. 水中じゃんけんをやりましょう。

10. 1,2の3で、同時に潜って、水中でじゃんけんをしてください。

11. 水中では、声は聞こえませんから、口を開いてはダメですよ。

12. 口を開いて、声を出そうとすると、水の飲みこんでしまいますよ。

13. 腕を使って、ジャンケンポンのリズムをとりますよ。

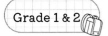 **Lesson 06**

 体育

P.E.

Grade 1 & 2

Swimming

Teacher

1. Alright, everyone's in. First, put your face in the water.

2. Keep your eyes opened while your face is in the water and hold your breath.

3. Raise both of your arms up and slowly bring down your arms straight to the water. Following the movement of your body, put your face in to the water.

4. Hold your breath while your face is in the water.

5. After your face is in the water, count to 10 and then look up.1, 2, 3, ...10!

6. OK, heads up.

7. You may feel scared when you get closer to the water with your eyes open, so try to open your eyes once your face is under the water.

8. Alright, face the person next to you.

9. We are going to play rock, scissors, paper in the water.

10. We are going to go into the water together on the count of three.

11. We can't hear your voice under the water so don't open your mouth.

12. If you do so then you might swallow water.

13. So, we will use our arms to keep the rhythm for the game.

中学年

水泳・水遊び

先生

1 これまでの学習を踏まえて、泳いでみましょう。

2 まずはバタ足を練習します。

3 はい、プールサイドに回ってください。

4 プールサイドに腰かけて、バタ足をしましょう。

プールの壁に足がぶつからないようにして、両足の足首が水面に出るくらい行いますよ。

5 はい！ピッ！

6 はい、そのまま、サブンとプールに入って。

今度は、プールの壁の方を向いて、壁に手を掛けて、顔をつけて体を浮かせて、

7 バタ足をしますよ。

8 ももの付け根からバタ足をします。膝をできるだけ曲げないようにして、行ってください。

息が続かなくなったら、一度、顔を上げて、プールの底に足をつけて、息を吸ったら、

9 またバタ足を始めますよ。

10 はい、では、全員、先生のいるプールサイドに集合して。プールから出ないでいいですよ。

11 そのままプールの中を歩いてきてください。はい、そろいましたね。

12 これ、知っていますね。ビート板といいます。

13 これはとても軽いので水に浮きます。

14 これを使って、反対のプールサイドまで泳いで行ってみましょう。

15 ビート板の丸くなった方を前にして、反対のまっすぐになっている方を両手で掴みます。

16 つかんだら、プールの壁を足で蹴って、顔を水に浸けた状態で、バタ足をして進みます。

息が続かなくなったら、止まって、息をして、そこからもう一回バタ足をしながら泳いで

17 いきますよ。

18 息をするとき、顔を水面から上げますね。

19 両手で顔をぬぐうと、ビート板が流れてしまいます。

20 ビート板から片手は離さないでください。

いいですね。早く行こうと焦らなくてもいいですけど、前に進もうとしてバタ足を

21 しないと、前に進みませんよ。

22 バタ足は太ももの付け根から動かしてキックするんですよ。

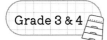
Grade 3 & 4

Swimming

Teacher

1 | Let's try to swim based on what we have learned so far.

2 | First, practice kicking your feet.

3 | Ok, please go around to the poolside.

4 | Sit on the side of the pool and start to kick your feet.

Put both legs in, so that they're just barely sticking out from the surface of the water and

5 | try not to hit the side of the pool. Ok, Beep!

6 | Now, go straight into the pool with a splash.

Now, face the wall of the pool, put your hands on the wall, put your face up to the wall,

7 | let your body float, and do flutter kicks.

8 | Start at the base of your thighs and try not to bend your knees as much as possible.

If you can't hold your breath, put your face is out of the water, then put your feet on the bottom

9 | of the pool, and breathe in. You can start kicking your feet again.

10 | Ok, now, all of you gather by the pool with me. You may not get out of the pool.

11 | Please go ahead and walk through the pool. Yes, we are all here.

12 | Do you know this? It is called a kick board.

13 | This is very light and floats in the water.

14 | Use this to swim to the opposite side of the pool.

With the rounded end of the kick board in front of you, hold the opposite straight end with

15 | both hands.

Once you hold the board, kick the pool wall with your feet and proceed to flutter kick with

16 | your face in the water.

If you can't keep holding your breath, stop and breathe in, and swim from there, kicking your feet

17 | once again.

18 | When you breathe, raise your face out of the water.

19 | If you wipe your face with both hands, the kick board will float away.

20 | Keep one hand on the kick board.

That's good. You don't have to rush to go fast, but if you don't flap your feet trying to move

21 | forward, you won't go forward.

22 | You have to move your foot from the base of your thigh to kick or flutter.

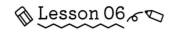
中学年

水泳・水遊び

先生

1 今日は、まず、かえる足キックを学習しましょう。

2 かえる足というくらいですから、足の動きはカエルの泳ぎに似ています。

3 水の中で、両足を曲げて、足の裏で伸ばしてキックして進みます。

4 かえる足キックは、よく聞かないとできませんよ。

5 みなさん、プールに入って、プルールサイドにつかまって、顔を水に浸けないで、先生の方を見て。

6 はい、体を浮かす。

7 両脚をそろえて伸ばし下さい。いいですねー。

8 それから、ももを、がに股になるように左右に開きながら、膝を曲げて、かかとをおしりへ

9 近づけます。いいですか。ここからですよ。

10 両足の足首を曲げて、足先を外側に向けてください。

11 足の裏が外に向いていますよ。

12 曲げ終わった足裏で水を後方へ押しやる気持ちで、強く斜め後ろに蹴って、内ももの力で水を挟み込むような気持ちで両脚をそろえます。

13 蹴った後はしばらく足を伸ばしたままにします。

14 もう一度やりますよ。

15 両足ががに股、かかとがお尻に着くくらい膝を曲げる。

16 足の裏で水をけって、両足をそろえて伸ばす。いいですかー。

17 では、ビート板をもってやってみましょうね。

18 顔は水面に出したままですよ。

19 皆さん、一度プールから上がってください。足の裏がうまく外を向いてないみたいですね。

20 いいですか、体をのばして、膝をついて正座の姿勢をして。

21 そうです。そうです。

22 はい、その状態で、アヒルすわりして。お尻を床にしっかりとつけて、両足の足の裏が上に来ていますね。

23 この状態で両足が曲がっていて、足の裏でキックするんですよ。

23 はい、もう一度プールに入って。

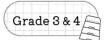 **Lesson 06**

体育

P.E.

Grade 3 & 4

Swimming

Teacher

1. Today we will first learn the frog leg kick.

2. They are called frog legs because the leg movements are similar to frogs swimming.

3. In the water, bend both legs, then stretch your feet straight, and kick to go forward.

4. You can't do the frog leg kick unless you listen carefully.

5. Everyone, please go into the pool, and hold on the sides. Keep your face out of the water, and look at the teacher.

6. Ok, now float your body.

7. Please put both legs together and stretch out. That's good.

8. Then, with your thighs spread apart, bend your knees so that your heels are close to your hips.

9. Okay, here we go. Here's what we're going to do.

10. Bend the ankles of both feet and point your toes outward.

11. The bottom of your feet are pointing outward!

12. Kick backward at an angle strongly with the bottom of the bent foot. As if pushing the water backward, and bring both legs together as if catching the water with the strength of your inner thighs.

13. After kicking, keep your legs stretch for a while.

14. We'll do it again.

15. Bend the knees so that both legs are bent at the hips and the heels touch your bottom.

16. Shake the water off with the bottom of your feet and stretch both feet together. Ready?

17. Now, let's try it with a kick board.

18. Keep your face above the water.

19. Everyone, please get out of the pool for a minute. It looks like the bottom of your feet are not facing outward properly.

20. Okay, stretch out and get into an upright sitting position on your knees.

21. That's right. That's right.

22. Yes, from there, sit like a duck. Your bottom is planted on the floor, and the bottom of both feet are facing upwards.

23. In this position, both legs are bent, and you kick with the soles of your feet. Okay, go into the pool again.

P.E.

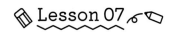

Lesson 07

体育

P.E.

低学年

機械運動

1

マット遊び

先生

今日の体育の授業は、雨なので、体育館で行います。体操服に着替えたら、

体育館に集合してください。開始のチャイムが鳴る前に、体育館に集合です。

時間がないので、急いで着替えてください。

今日は、マットを使った運動をおこないます。6年生のお兄さんとお姉さんが、

手伝ってくれますから、倉庫から、マットを運んできましょう。

各列に2枚ずつ、運んでください。

6年生の皆さん、マットは、縦に隙間がないようにくっつけてください。

1年生は、少しの隙間でも指を挟んだりしますから。

では、今日は、マット運動に慣れるために、みんなで、丸太棒になって、

ゴロゴロ転がるところから始めます。

マットの上で、気をつけの姿勢で、両方の腕を挙げて、手のひらをくっつけて、

自分が丸太棒になります。

丸太棒になったら、ゴロゴロとマットの端まで転がっていき、端まで着いたら、

起き上がって列に戻ってきてください。

あまり早く転がると、後で目が回りますから、ゆっくりと回ってくださいね。

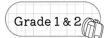
  Gymnastics 1

Mat Exercises

Teacher

1 Since it's raining today, we are going to have our class indoor. After you change into your P.E. outfit please come to the gym. We will gather before the bell rings, so please change quickly.

2 Today, we are going to do some exercises using the exercise mats. 6th-grade students will be helping you bring the exercise mats over from the storage.

3 Bring two mats for each row.

4 6th-graders, I want you to put the mats together side by side and make sure there is no space in between.

5 1st-grade students can easily get their fingers stuck in small spaces.

6 Today, I want you all to get used to the mat exercises so we are going to start off by rolling like a log.

7 On the mat, lie down with your body straight both arms up and your palms touching together looking like a log.

8 Then, start rolling to the end of the mat. After you reach to the end of the mat , stand up and go back to your row.

7 If you roll too fast, you may get dizzy, so roll slowly.

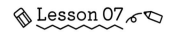

体育

P.E.

中学年

機械運動

マット遊び

先生

1 マットを2列に引いてください。

2 前転の練習から行いましょう。

3 足をそろえて気をつけの姿勢をして、両手をついて頭の後ろをマットにつけて くるっと回って、素早く、かかとを引きよせてしゃがみ立ちをします。

4 回転を速くして、頭を前かがみに突出しさないと立ち上がれませんよ。

5 そう、そうやって勢いをつけて立ち上がってください。

6 では、次に後転の練習をしましょう。

7 はい、後ろ向きにしゃがんで、あごを引いて背中を丸めますよ。

8 ひじを締めて、耳の横に両手を手のひらを上にして、くるっと回転して両手でマットを 突き放して、しゃがみ立ちしますよ。

9 回転したあと、もっと体に足を引き寄せておかないと、丸みが足りませんよ。

10 今日はさらに大技に挑戦しましょう。

11 見ていてください。

12 後転をして、足を開いて立ち上がります。

13 背中がマットについたら、両足を広げて、両手でマットを押してたちがりますよ。

14 はい、できるだけ足は広げてマットの外に着地しますよ。

15 マット一枚だと高さが足りないから、開脚して立ち上がるのは難しいかな。それじゃあ、 マットを3枚重ねてください。

16 そうしたら、開脚立するとき、高さがあるので簡単に立ち上がれます。

Gymnastics

Mat Exercises

Grade 3 & 4

Teacher

1. Please spread the P.E mats in two lines.

2. Let's start by practicing forward rolls.

3. With your feet together in position, put your hands on the mat, turn around with the back of your head on the mat, and quickly pull your heels back to a crouching position.

4. You need to spin faster and stick your head forward or you cannot stand up.

5. Yes, that's how you get up with momentum.

6. Now let's practice the backward roll.

7. Now squat backward and round your back with your chin pulled back.

8. Tighten your elbows, put your hands palm up next to your ears, spin around and push off the mat with both hands, and stand up in a crouch.

9. After you rotate, you need to pull your legs more into your body, otherwise you will not be round enough.

10. Today, let's try an even bigger move.

11. Watch.

12. Do a backward roll and stand up with your legs open.

13. Once your back is on the mat, spread your legs apart and push off the mat with both hands.

14. You will land on the outside of the mat with your legs spread as wide as possible.

15. If one mat is not high enough for you to stand up, or it's difficult to spread your legs then, please pile up three mats on top of each other.

16. If the mats are higher, it will be easier to open your legs when you stand.

機械運動

マット遊び

高学年

先生

1　マット運動も、すでに前転や後転は皆さん出来るようになりましたから、さらに大きな
2　前転や足を開いた開脚後転などレベルをあげていきましょう。

3　まず、大きな前転からやってみましょう。
4　両手をできるだけ遠くに着きながら、両足で強く蹴って、膝の伸ばして回転したら、
5　かかとを素早く引付けて、立ち上がります。
6　立ちあがったら、気をつけの姿勢になります。
7　指先まで伸びて、体の横についているときれいに見えます。
8　両足は揃えます。そしたらすぐにマットから降りてください。

9　飛び込み前転をやってみましょう。
　　両足で踏み切って、飛び込むようにして腰を大きく開いて、両手でマットに着手して、
10　体を受け止めて、顎を引いて、体を丸くして前転します。

11　体育係の人、1名用具室から縄跳びを一本持ってきてください。
12　では、体育係の人にマットの両側から、縄跳びを張ってもらいます。
13　この高さから少しづつなれるようにしていきましょう。
14　着手した後、タイミングよく、首、背中、腰、足の順に接地させることが大事です。

15　では、次に、後転をやりましょう。
16　開脚後転といって、回転した後に足を開いて立ち上がりますよ。
　　では、しゃがみ立ちして、後ろまわりして、足先が頭を越したら、足を開き、
17　手の近くに足を受けます。

18　最後に両手で、マットを押して開脚立します。
　　そうです。そうです。では、しゃがまないで、立ったままからの開脚後転に
19　挑戦してみましょう。要領は同じですよ。
20　後ろ向きに立って、しゃがむというところが増えてただけです。
21　では、やってみますよ。

Gymnastics

Mat Exercises

Teacher

1 Now that everyone can do forward and backward rotations on the mat, let's move up to

2 the next level, and try things like big forward rotations and open-leg backward rotations.

3 First, let's start with a big forward rotation.

4 Put your hands as far forward as possible and kick the ground hard with both feet.

5 Stretch your knees far and when you flip and your heel touch the ground, stand up immediately.

6 When you get up, you should be standing straight.

7 It looks good and proper when your fingers are straight and your arms are at the side of your body.

8 Both feet should be together. After that please get off the mat immediately.

9 Let's try a jumping forward rotation.

Step off with both feet and open your hips wide as you dive forward. Touch the ground with

both hands, absorbing all the energy of your body, pull your jaw in and then rotate by folding

10 your body forward.

11 One of the sports prefects, can you bring a jump rope from the equipment room?

12 Now, I would like the sports prefect to stretch the jump rope from both sides of the mat.

13 Let's start from this height and gradually get used to it.

14 Once you land, it is important to land in the order of neck, back, hips, and then feet.

15 Next, let's try a backward rotation.

16 This is called an open-leg backward rotation, as you stand up with your legs open after rotating.

Now, squat down and turn around. When your toes go over your head, open your legs and

17 bring them near your hands.

18 Finally, press the mat with both of your hands and stand up with your legs open.

That's right. Very good. Now let's try an open-leg backward rotation from a standing position

19 without squatting. It is the same as before.

20 The only difference is that we have added the part where we stand backward and squat down.

21 Let's give it a try.

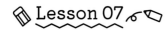

高学年

機械運動
マット遊び

 3

先生 📢

1 では、ちょっと難しいマット運動に取り組んでみましょう。

2 側方倒立回転という運動です。

3 先生も上手ではないので、ビデオでどんな運動か見てみましょう。

4 テレビを持ってきましたら、見ましょう。

5 はい、その場で腰を下ろしてください。はい、回しますよ。

6 ビデオをコマ送りにして、説明をしますね。

7 まず、体が斜めになって立っていますね。両手を上げてバンザイしています。

8 次です、ここ。手の位置に注意してください。左手から着いて右手を着いていますが、その時、左手と右手は横に並んでいて、体が正面斜めだったのに、横向きになるようにねじっていますね。

9 そして真横で逆立ちして、次に、回転して、左手をマットから離して、左足で着地して、横向きに起き上がっています。

10 この運動ができるには、逆立ち、倒立という、腕で立つ動作の感覚がつかめていないと難しいです。

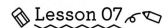

体育

Grade 5 & 6

Gymnastics

Mat Exercises

Teacher

1 | Now, Let's move on to a more difficult mat exercise.

2 | It is an exercise called a cartwheel.

3 | I'm not very good at it myself, so let's watch the video to see what kind of exercise it is.

4 | Let's watch it after I bring the TV.

5 | OK, please sit down where you are. I'm going to start the video now.

6 | Let me show you the video bit by bit while I explain.

7 | First, he is standing with his body at an angle, with both his hands up.

Next, here. Note the position of his hands. He lands on his left hand first, then his right hand.

At this time, when the left and right hands are next to each other and his body is facing forward,

8 | he turns his body sideways.

After facing sideways on his hands for a second, he rotates , releases his left hand, lands on his

9 | left foot and brings his body up.

In order to be able to do this movement, you need to master the handstand or standing upside

10 | down, which is basically like standing on your arms.

P. E.

高学年

機械運動

逆立ち

先生 📣

1 　まず、逆立ちを練習してみましょうね。後ろ足で床を蹴り上げて、両足をまっすぐ 上に上げて逆立ちします。顔が床を向いてますね。これが逆立ちです。

2 　では、みんなで逆立ちの練習をしますよ。

3 　3人一組で練習しますから、全体3列になります。横の3名が一組です。 一人が逆立ちをして、後の二人が左右から足を支えてあげます。

4 　足を支えたら、3つ数えて、足を前に押し出して、着地できるようにしてあげてください。 人によっては、手を床に付けた状態から逆立ちするのが難しいことがあります。 この場合は、前まわりのように、勢いをつけて足を跳ね上げてください。

5 　はい、次、交代して練習して下さい。

6 　はじめてだから、なかなかうまくいきませんね。全員先生の所に集まって。 いいですか、目をつぶって。万歳をして。逆立ちをしているイメージをしてください。

7 　手の上に床がありますよ。もっと両腕をピンと伸ばさないと体重を支えられません。

8 　肘は曲げないで。いいですか。そのイメージで、逆立ちをしますよ。

9 　はい、手を下して、目を開けて、また3人一組になって、練習してください。

10 　では、側方倒立回転の練習に移ります。ビデオを思い出してくださいね。

11 　最初から真横を向いた状態でマットに手をついても側転はできません。

12 　進行方向に向かって横向きに立つのではなく、前向きに足を前後に開いて立ち、思いっきり バンザイして、おしりを曲げながら手を下ろし始めます。前足の順番で移動させます。

13 　手を着いている時は横向きの逆立ち（開脚）と同じで、できるだけバンザイ（背伸び）を しておきます。

14 　後ろ足を着地させるときは、最初の前を向くの逆の考え方で腰を折り曲げながら、 身体は後ろを向き起き上がるときに横を向くようにすると簡単です。

15 　腰の折れ具合は着手まで前向き→着手中は伸ばして横向き→起き上がり時は後ろ向きと 変化します。

16 　側転は柔軟性が無いと難しい運動です。

17 　特に開脚で足を広げるので前屈と股関節の柔軟性が必要です。

18 　足を拡げて開脚する練習をしてください。 また、身体を支える上半身の筋力が必要ですので、先日も学習した腕立て伏せや腹筋を

19 　毎日少しずつ練習して下さい。

Grade 5 & 6

Gymnastics
Exercise Mat Handstand

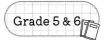

Teacher
📢

1 First, let's practice a handstand. Kick off from the floor with your back foot and stand upside down with both legs straight. Your face should be facing the floor. This is the handstand. OK.

2 Now we are going to practice handstands together.

We are going to do it in groups of three. Let's get into three lines. The three people beside you are your group members. One of you should try to do a handstand, and the other two will

3 support your legs from both sides.

Once the legs are supported, count to three and push the legs forward so that the person can land on the ground. Some may have difficulty standing upside down with their hands on the

4 floor. In this case, please use momentum to bounce their feet up, as before.

5 Good. Next, please take turns practicing.

6 Since this is your first time, it's not going to be easy. Everyone, gather around me.

OK, Close your eyes. Raise your hands and imagine you are standing on your head. You have

7 your hands on the floor. You need to extend your arms more to support your weight.

8 Don't bend your elbows. Okay, keep that image and let's try a real handstand.

9 OK, put your hands down, open your eyes, and practice again in groups of three.

10 Now let's move on to the cartwheel. Please remember the video.

11 Even if you touch the mat with your hands facing straight, you cannot roll sideways.

Instead of standing sideways facing the direction you will travel, stand forward with one foot in front of the other. Raise your hands as high as you can, and begin to lower your hands while

12 bending at the hips. Move your front foot first.

Then go on your hands, it is the same as handstand sideways with open legs, but keep your

13 hands stretched out as much as possible.

When landing it is easier to bend your waist first, in the opposite direction of the first motion,

14 so that the body is facing backward and then sideways when rising.

The position of the hips depends on the position of the body. It is forward facing until the hands are on the ground. While reaching down, it is extended and sideways.Then it changes to

15 backward-facing when getting up.

16 The cartwheels are difficult exercises if you are not flexible.

17 In particular, because the legs are widely spread, it is generally necessary to have joint flexibility.

18 Practice spreading your legs and feet.

In addition, upper body muscle strength to support the body is necessary.

19 So please practice push-ups and train your abs little by little, as we have already learned.

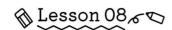

Lesson 08

低学年

走って、跳んで遊ぼう

先生

1 今日は、「どんどん走って、跳んでみよう」をやりましょう。

2 では、まず2列に並んでください。番号！

3 では、偶数番号の人は、前の人の横に並んでください。

4 では、ピッ。

5 では、4人ずつ順番に、あの木まで走って、木を回って戻ってきます。

6 戻ってきたら、列の後ろに並んでください。

7 では、次に、木との間に、段ボールを置きますから、そこを跳んで、木を回ってきてください。

8 今日は、よく走りましたね。走った後は、整理運動をしっかりしておかないと、足の筋肉をつることがありますから、整理運動をします。

9 では、全員、「前へーならへ！」両手を肩の高さでまっすぐ横に開いて、

10 隣とぶつからないように広がれ、ピッ！

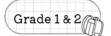

Lesson 08

Running and Jumping

Teacher

1　Today, we are going to run and jump a lot.

2　First, make two rows. Number call!

3　Now, those of you with even numbers, please line up next to the person in front of you.

4　OK, (whistle).

5　Alright, I want groups of four to run to the tree over there and come back.

6　Once you return, go to the back of the line.

7　Next, I'm going to set a cardboard box between the trees and you need to go over it and then go around the tree.

8　We ran a lot today. After you run, we need to do cool down exercises. Otherwise, you will get a cramp in your leg so let's cool down now.

9　OK, everyone, line up, face forward! Spread your arms to the level of your shoulders.

10　Spread out so you don't bump into the people next to you.

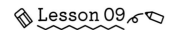
跳の運動

中学年

先生

1 今日は、走りながら跳ぶという運動を行います。

2 用具係は、段ボールの箱を持ってきて、2列に並べます。

3 はい、一個目はここに並べてください。

4 次は1，2，3，ハイ、ここ、次は一個目と2個目と同じ間隔で置いてください。

5 では、今日の運動を説明します。
走りながら、この箱を飛び越え、また走って次の箱を飛び越して、

6 走って飛び越していきます。

7 4つとも飛び越えたら、駆け足で戻ってきて、列の後ろに並んでください。

8 では、練習してみますよ。

9 先頭の人、走って飛んでみてください。

先生

1 こういう時はリズムを付けて走ります。

2 見てください。トン、トン、トーン。トーンで飛びます。

3 いいですか、まず、このリズムを練習します。

4 段ボールの箱を飛ばないで、その横を走りますよ。
では、先頭の人、ハイ、トン、トン、そこで飛び越す、はい、トン、トン、そこで飛び越す、

5 いいですよ。リズムが取れてきました。はい、次の列の人。

6 もう少し、歩幅を広げないと、リズムに乗りませんよ。

7 少し大股にするつもりで、はい、慣れてきましたね、

8 では、走るスピードを速くしますよ。はい、では、いよいよ、実際に段ボールを飛び越えて

9 走ってみましょう。練習ですから、スピードが遅くても構いません。

10 リズムにのって、走って飛び越す、走って飛び越していきますよ。
このリズムで、走って跳ぶという動作が上手にできるようになると、もっと楽しい運動が

11 できるようになります。

12 では、もう少し段ボールの高さを高くしましょう。

13 段ボールの箱を立ててください。

14 段ボールの中には重しとして石が入れてありますが、石が段ボールを傷つけないで底に

15 転がれるように、ゆっくりとやってくださいね

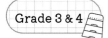

体育

Grade 3 & 4

Jumping

Teacher

1. Today we will be doing an exercise called running and jumping.
2. Sports prefect, please bring cardboard boxes and arrange them in two rows.
3. Yes, the first one should be placed here.
4. Next, 1, 2, 3, ok, here, next, place them at the same spacing as the first and second.
5. Now let me explain today's exercise.

   First run and jump over this box, then run again and jump over the next box, then run and
6. jump over the next box, and so on.
7. Once you have jumped over all four, run back and get to the back of the line.
8. Okay, let's try to practice.
9. The first person, try to run and jump.

Teacher

1. In these situations, Try to run with a rhythm.
2. Look at me. Stomp, stomp, stomp and jump.
3. Okay, first, we will practice this rhythm.
4. At first, don't jump over the cardboard box, let's run beside it.

   Now, the first person, stomp, stomp and jump, again, stomp, stomp and jump, okay.
5. You are getting into the rhythm. Yes, next person in line.
6. If you don't widen your stride a little more, you won't get into the rhythm.
7. You're going to have to make it a little bigger, alright. You are getting used to it.
8. Now, let's start running faster. Yes, now it's time to actually run and jump over the cardboard.
9. Since this is a practice exercise, it does not matter if your running speed is slow.
10. You'll get into the rhythm, run and jump over, run and jump over.

    This rhythm will make the exercise more enjoyable as you become more proficient at running
11. and jumping.
12. Now let's raise the height of the cardboard a little more.
13. Stand up the cardboard boxes.
14. There is a stone in the cardboard we use as a weight, so please move the box slowly so
15. that the stone can roll to the bottom without damaging the cardboard.

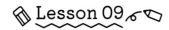
跳の運動

中学年

先生

全員整列したら、駆け足で砂場に来ます。はい、ピッ。

今日は走り幅飛びの練習をします。

走り幅跳びとは、勢いをつけてジャンプして、できるだけ遠くに飛ぶ運動です。

まずは、跳び箱の踏み台まで走って踏み台から飛ぶという練習をします。

踏み台までは5歩で走ります。

そして、利き足大体の人は右足だと思いますが、利き足で踏み台から前に飛び上がります。

それから、両足で着地します。その時は体を曲げて両足で着地します。その時の姿勢は、

「くの字ではなく、膝を曲げて、「ん」の字です。

踏み台を飛び出したら、空中で両足をそろえないと、両足着地できません。

では、踏切台を外してください。

砂場にフープを置きますから、白線からそのフープの中への着地を狙ってジャンプして下さい。

では、だれが一番遠くまで飛べるが競争しましょう。

用具係の二人は、とんだ距離を測る係をやってください。

いいですか。ルールを説明します。

白線より前に出てはいけません。白線までで踏み切ります。

白線より前に出たら失格です。

着地までの距離は、着地した時に着いた手、おしり、足等一番短いところで測ります。

一人2回ずつ跳んで良い方の記録をその人の記録とします。

では始めますよ。

Jumping

Grade 3 & 4

Teacher

1. Once we are all lined up, we are going to run to the sandbox. Ok, beep.

2. Today we will practice long jump.

3. The long jump is an exercise in which you run and jump as far as possible.

4. First, let's practice running to the step and jumping off.

5. Try to run there in 5 steps.

6. Then, jump forward with your dominant foot, which I think is the right foot for most people, and land on both feet. When landing bend your body and land on both feet. The posture at that time is not the "ku" Hiragana character, but bend your knees and make the "n" character.

7. Now, the first student in the line, please practice. When you jump off the step, you must keep both feet together in the air to land on both feet.

8. Now, please remove the step.

7. Now we will place a hula hoop in the sandbox, so now jump from the white line to the inside of the hula hoop.

10. Let's compete to see who can jump the furthest.

11. The two sports prefect should be measuring the distance.

12. OK. Let me explain the rules.

13. Do not step out before the white line. Step out in the white line.

14. If you get ahead of the white line, you have failed.

15. The distance to landing is measured at the shortest point where the hand, hip, foot, or any body part landed on the ground.

16. Each person will jump twice and we will keep the better score.

17. Let's begin.

走の運動

中学年

先生

　今日から、グラウンドのトラックを、みんなでジョギングします。2列のままで先生の合図に合わせて走ってください。

走る時は、1，2，3，4と掛け声を掛けながら走りますよ。

はい、ピッ！3周します。

1，2，3，4，2，2，3，4

はい、その場で駆け足、はい、足踏み。

全体とまれ。

これまでいつも直線で走っていましたが、トラックを回って走る練習をします。

それからバトンの練習をします。

直線を走る時とコーナーを走る時の走り方は違います。

　直線を走る時は、つま先で走り、手はパーにして、腕は大きく直角に振って、前を向いて走ります。

　コーナーを走る時は、小刻みな歩幅で、足の回転を速くして、体を少し内側に倒して、外に膨らまないようにして走ります。

いいですか、走りながらそれを体で覚えていきますよ。

直線25mを走り、コーナーを回って、更に直線を25m走ります。

直線は全力、コーナーはできるだけ内側を回り、直線でまた全力で走ります。

用具係はゴールの所に線を引いて来て下さい。

2列で、二人ずつ練習をします。ゴールしたら、戻ってきてください。

最初の二人準備して下さい。

よーい、ピッ！次、よーい、ピッ！

Running Exercises

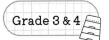

Teacher
📢

From today, we will all jog around the track on the school grounds, staying in two lines and running according to the teacher's commands.

When you run, call out "1, 2, 3, 4".

Ok, beep! Three laps.

1, 2, 3, 4, 2, 2, 3, 4

Yes, now run on the spot. Yes, then slow down and march on the spot.

Now everyone please stop.

We have always ran in a straight line, but today we will practice running around the track.

Then, we will practice passing a baton.

The way you run in a straight line is different from the way you run around a corner.

When you run in a straight line, run on your toes, hands in par, arms swinging at large right angles, facing forward.

When you run around corner, take small strides, turn your feet quickly, and run with your body slightly inward and not running outward.

Look, your body will lean when you run.

We will run 25 meters in a straight line, turn a corner, and then run another 25 meters in a straight line.

Run as fast as you can in a straight line, go around corners as far inside as possible, and then run as fast as you can again in a straight line.

Sports prefect please come to the finish line and draw a line at the goal.

Practice in two lines, two people at a time. When you reach the finish line, come back.

Okay, the first two students please get ready.

Ready set, beep! Next pair, ready set, beep!

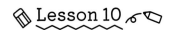

Lesson 10

走の運動

中学年

先生

1 バトンの手渡しの練習をします。

2 走りながらバトンを渡す、前を向いたまま、バトンをもらうというのは難しいことです。

3 縦に２列になっていますが、まず、縦４列に並びます。

4 偶数番号の人、右側に出る。ピッ。

5 一歩前に出る。ピッ。全体、右向け右。ピッ！

6 列と列の間を少し開けます。

7 用具係は、列の後ろの人にバトンを渡して下さい。

8 まず、感触をつかみますよ。前の人に左手で渡す。

9 前の人は右手でもらって、左手に持ちかえる。

10 同じように前の人に渡します。

11 渡す人、もらう人の手の位置は平行になるようにします。

12 先頭の列にバトンが渡ったら、全員、回れ右して、後ろを向いて、同じようにバトンの手渡しを練習します。

13 はい、ピッ、はい、ピッ、はい、ピッ、回れ―右。はい、ピッ、はい、ピッ。

14 分かりましたか。では走りながらバトンを渡す練習をします。

15 ４列のまま、直線コースに移動して下さい。10メートルおきに並んでください。

16 では、一番後ろの人が走りながら前の人に渡しますよ。

17 前の人は、後ろの人が3m位までに近づいてきたら、右腕を後ろに出して、手のひらを上にて、後ろの人がバトンを渡しやすいように、右腕を動かさないようにして走り出します。

18 後ろを見る必要はありませんよ。前を見て走ります。

19 ゆっくり走しろうとせず、全力で走りださないと、走ってきた後ろの人に追いつかれてしまって、ぶつかってしまします。
後ろの人は走ってきていますから勢いがついていますが、前の人は今から走りだしますし、右腕を後ろに伸ばしていますから、速度が遅いです。

20 もちろん、余り早く走り出してはいけません。最初は、走りだすタイミングがつかめないと思いますが、徐々にわかってきますからね。

21 後ろの人は、左腕を伸ばし、前の人の手にバトンを押し込むように渡します。

22 だから、走ってきたコースを右に曲げて、前の人の右側を走り抜けるようにします。
バトンを渡したら、その場で少しまっすぐに駆け足します。

23 突然、コースから外れようとしないでください。他のバトンをしている人たちにぶつかってしまいます。

Grade 3 & 4

Running Exercises

Teacher

1. Let's practice passing the baton.

2. It is difficult to pass the baton while running, looking forward, and receiving the baton.

3. Now you are in two lines but let's make four.

4. Even-numbered people, step to the right. Beep!

5. Now step forward. Beep! Everyone, turn right. Beep!

6. Open the space between the two lines slightly.

7. Sports prefect, please pass the baton to the students at the back of the line.

8. First, get a feel for it first. Pass it to the person in front of you with your left hand.

9. The person in front of you receives it with their right hand, and then changes it to their left hand.

10. Pass it to the person in front of you in the same way.

11. The hands of the person passing and the hands of the person receiving should be parallel.

12. After the baton is passed to the first row, everyone should turn around, and practice handing the baton again.

13. Ok, beep! Ok, beep! Ok, beep! Turn-right. Yes, beep! Ok, beep!

14. You, see? Now we will practice passing the baton while running.

15. Keep the 4 lines and move in a straight line. Please line up every 10 meters.

16. Now, the person at the end of the line will pass it to the person in front as you run. When the person behind you comes about 3 meters to you, put your right arm out behind your back, palm up, so that the person behind can easily pass the baton to you.

17. Without moving your right arm, start to run.

18. You don't need to look behind you. Look forward ahead of you and run.

19. If you don't start running as fast as you can instead of trying to run slowly, the person behind you will catch up to you and you will bump into them. The person behind you is running, so they are already going fast enough, but the person in front of you is starting to run now, and your right arm is extended behind you, so your speed is slow.

20. Of course, do not start running too quickly. At first, you may not know when to start running, but you will gradually figure it out.

21. The person in the back extend your left arm and pass the baton to the person in front of you pushing it into their hand.

22. So, bend to the right on the course you have been running and try to run through on the right side of the person in front of you. After passing the baton, run a little straighter on the spot.

23. Do not suddenly try to get out from the course otherwise you will bump into other people passing the baton.

高学年

機械運動

跳び箱

先生

1 今日からは跳び箱の学習をします。

2 跳び箱は、もともとは馬跳びとういう遊びが起源です。

3 実際にみんなで馬跳びをやってみましょう。

4 4列で行います。

5 各列の先頭の人は両腕が隣と人と当たらないように広がってください。

6 各列、右向け右。

7 今から馬跳びの説明をします。

8 先頭の人は、次の人から順番に飛び越えて、飛び越え終わったら、並んで馬になります。

9 最後の人が飛び終わったら集合して下さい。

10 跳び方と馬になる場合の注意を説明します。

11 馬になる時は、前かがみになって、膝を曲げて、膝の上に手を置いて、飛ぶ人の体重を支えられるようにします。

12 跳ぶ人は、背中に両手を着いて頭に当たらないように両足を広げて飛び越えます。

13 はい、では、跳び箱を飛んでみましょう。

14 各列の前から4人で、跳び箱をそれぞれ、上3段持ってきてください。

15 上から3段目の前と後ろの穴が開いている持ち手から手を入れて、2人で持って、あとの二人は、横を片手で持って、もう一方の手は跳び箱の上に添えて動かないようにして、持ってきてください。

16 前を持つ人は、跳び箱の方を向いて後ろ向きで歩かないでくださいね。

17 転びます。前を向いて後ろ手に運びますよ。

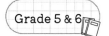
Grade 5 & 6

Gymnastics

Vaulting

Teacher

1 | From today we are going to learn about vaulting.

2 | The origin of vault comes from the children's activity "horse jumping."

3 | Let's actually try horse jumping together.

4 | Please get into four lines.

5 | The first person in each line should spread out your arms to make enough space so that you are not touching the person next to you.

6 | Each row, please turn right.

7 | I will now explain horse jumping.

8 | The first person in each row will jump over the people in your row one by one.

When you have finished jumping over everyone, please line up and become a horse.

9 | When the last person has finished jumping, please regroup.

10 | Here are some instructions on how to jump and what to expect when becoming a horse.

11 | When you become a horse, you should be bent forward, knees bent, and hands on the knees so that you can support the weight of the person jumping.

12 | The person jumping should jump over with your hands on the horse's back. Spread your legs apart to avoid hitting the horse's head.

13 | Let's jump over the vault.

14 | Starting with the four people in the front row, please bring vaulting boxes from the top three tiers.

15 | Two people should hold the top three tiers by putting their hands in through the handles with holes in the front and back, and the other two people should hold the sides with one hand, and rest the other hand on the top of the vault to keep it still.

16 | Make sure that the person at the front is not facing the vault and walking backward.

17 | If you do that you will fall. You should face forward and hold the vault behind you.

Lesson 11

体育

P.E.

機械運動
跳び箱

先生

では、順番に跳び箱を飛んでみましょう。

跳び箱が跳べるようなるには、3つのポイントがあります。

1つ目は手の位置、

2つ目は肩の位置、

3つ目はお尻の高さです。

手は跳び箱の前方に着くようにします。肩は腕より前方にくるようにします。

お尻はできるだけ高い位置です。

お尻の位置が高いことにより、肩の位置も前に出しやすく、跳び箱の上部との空間にも余裕があるため跳び越しやすくなります。

これらをうまくやるためには、助走に勢いをつけて、ロイター版を両足で強く踏み切ることが必要です。

踏み込んで手を着いたら、肩が手より前になるようにしますよ。

強く踏み込んで、お尻を高くしないと肩が前に来ません。

腕を大きく振り上げて、手で跳び箱を思いっきりパンと叩いたら体がフワと持ち上がります。

体育

P.E.

Gymnastics

Vaulting

Teacher

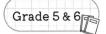

1. Now, let's take turns jumping the vault.

2. There are three key points to master

3. The first is the position of the hands,

4. The second is the position of the shoulders,

5. The third is the height of the hips.

6. Your hands should be in front of the vault. Shoulders should be in front of the arms.

7. The hips should be as high as possible.

The higher the hips are, the easier it is to move the shoulders forward, and the more space

8. there is between the hips and the top of the vault, the easier it is to jump over the vault.

In order to do these well, you need to have momentum in the run up and step strongly off

9. the spring board with both feet.

10. When you step in and reach with your hands, make sure your shoulders are in front of your hands.

11. If you don't step off strongly and raise your hips, then your shoulders will not come forward.

If you swing your arms up in the air and slap the vault with your hands   as hard as you can,

12. your body will lift up.

P.E.

ボール運び

低学年

先生

1 今日は、ボールを使った運動をしましょう。

2 男子2列、女子2列の列を作ります。

3 まず、男女それぞれ一列に並んでください。

4 はい、並んだら、前から順番に、番号を言ってください。

5 では、偶数の番号の人は、列の左にずれてください。

6 偶数ってわかりますか。

7 番号が 2,4,6,8,10…この番号の人は、左側にずれてくださいね、いいかな。

8 次に、偶数の人は、一歩前にでて、奇数の人と一列になってください。

9 これで、男子が2列、女子が2列になりました。

それでは、男子の左の列と女子の右の列は、それぞれ、外に向かって、先生の笛に合わせて、広がってください。笛を吹くのをやめたら、そこに止まって、前を向いて、整列します。

10 はい、ピ、ピ・・

11 では、各列の先頭の人は、それぞれ、ボールを取りに来てください。

12 よいですかー。今から。ボールリレーを行います。

13 皆さん、腕を挙げて、前の人から、頭の上でボールをもらって、後ろの人に回します。

最後の人は、ボールを受け取ったら、前の人に、同じように、頭の上でボールを戻していきます。

15 上半身を伸ばして、ぐっと、後ろに反ってください。

16 後ろの人が、ボールを両手で挟んだら、手を放します。

Ball Games

Teacher

1 Today, we are going to play a ball game.

2 We are going to make two lines of boys and two lines of girls.

3 First, boys and girls make one line each.

4 Once you are all lined up, we'll do a headcount starting from the front.

5 If you are an even number, please step to the left of your row.

6 Do you all know what even numbers are?

7 They are numbers like 2, 4, 6, 8, 10... So those of you who are even numbers step to your left, OK?

8 Next, those with even numbers, I want you to step forward and then form a line with those who are odd numbers.

9 Now we have two lines each of boys and girls.

Alright, so the left row of the boy's row and the left row of the girl's row, please walk outwards as I blow the whistle. Once I stop blowing the whistle, stop and line up straight again.

10 (Beep! Beep!)

11 OK, great. The first person of each row please come and pick up the ball.

12 Ready? We are going to have a relay using the ball.

13 Put your arms up. We are going to pass the ball above your head to the person behind you until it gets all way to the back.

14 Once it gets to the last person, pass the ball forward doing the same thing

15 Just stretch your upper-body and lean back.

16 And once the person behind you receives the ball with both hands, you can let go of the ball.

体育

P.E.

高学年

球技運動

バレーボール説明

先生

1 今日からボールを使った球技運動をします。

2 いろんな球技をやりますが、今回はバレーボールをやります。

3 バレーは、床に白い線が引いてあってコートができていますね。

4 そのコートの間にネットを張って、ネット挟んでボールを打ち合うゲームです。

5 バレーボールは、9人制、6人制によるチーム制で、チームで協力して、コート内でボールを床に落とさないで、繋いで、3回以内で相手側のコートに戻すというのが基本ルールのゲームです。

6 ドッチボールとはやり方もルールも違います。

7 では、ルールを説明します。

8 今回は、3人バレーボールを練習します。3人でチームを作ります。

9 まず、2つのチームでじゃんけんをして、勝ったチームの一人が、コートの後ろのラインの外から、サーブと言って、ボールをこぶしで打って相手のコートに入れます。

10 相手は、ボールが飛んで来たら、レシーブと言って、ボールを床に落とさないようにして打って、仲間につなぎます。

11 ボールをもらったら、トスと言って、ボールをネット近くに高く上げます。

12 そしたらもう一人が、飛び上がってネットに体や腕が当たらないようにしながら、ボールを相手のコートに打ち返します。

13 相手は、打ち返されてきたボールを、同じようにレシーブ、トス、アタックで戻します。

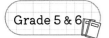 **Lesson 13**

Ball Sports

Grade 5 & 6

Volleyball

1

Teacher

1. Today we are going to play a ball game.

2. We will play many different types of ball games, but this time we will play volleyball.

3. To play volleyball, we use a court with white lines drawn on the floor.

4. We place a net in the middle of the court and the players play by hitting the ball across the net.

5. There are nine or six player-teams in volleyball. The basic rule is that teams must work together to send the ball back to the opponent's side of the court within three passes and without dropping the ball on the floor.

6. It is different from dodgeball, both in the way it is played and in the rules.

7. Now, let me explain the rules.

8. This time, we will practice 3-player volleyball, and we will form teams of three.

9. First, the two teams will play rock-paper-scissors. One member of the winning team will serve from outside the line at the back of the court. A serve is when you hit the ball with your fist into the opponent's court.

10. When the ball comes into your court, you should say "receive" and hit the ball without dropping it on the floor. The ball is then passed to the other player.

11. After receiving the ball, the player tosses the ball and raises it high near the net.

12. The other player then jumps up and hits the ball back to the other player's court, making sure not to hit the net with your body or arms.

13. The opponent then receives, tosses, and attacks the ball back in the same way.

高学年

球技運動

バレーボール説明

先生

1. 3回でなくても構いません。
2. 1回目とか2回目で相手のコートに返してもいいんですが、それだと、
3. ボールに触れない人が出てきてしまうでしょ。
4. だから、私たちの学年では、原則3回目で相手方のコートに返すというルールにします。

5. 次にボールの打ち方の説明をしますね。サーブからです。
6. ボールを左手にもって、ネットの正面になるように立って、足をまげて中腰になってください。
7. そうです。右足を引いてください。
8. 右手をこぶしにして、手のひら側を上に向けておきます。
9. 左手に持ったボールを肩の高さくらいまで上に上げて、落ちてきたボールの下の部分を右のこぶしと手首のあたりで、すくうように打って、相手側のコートに入れます。
10. はい、上手ですね。
11. 次はレシーブです。
12. 両手をクの字にして両腕とも伸ばしたまま併せてください。

13. これで肩から手まで、三角形の形になりますね。
14. この三角形の中で、さっき田中さんが打ってくれたボールを打ち返して、チームの人につなぎます。
15. 体は中腰にして、足は両方平行にして、構えてください。
16. ボールは肩より低い位置で取ります。
17. ボールを受ける瞬間、しっかりとヒジを伸ばして、両腕で作った三角形の面でボールを受けることが大切です。どうしてかわかりますか。
18. この時に腕が下がると、ボールをとらえる時に腕を振ってしまい、ボールのコントロールができません。
19. 伸ばした腕と前の足の太腿が平行になるイメージでボールをとらえます。

20. ひざが伸びきって、立ち上がったままボールの落下地点に移動すると、あごもあがって、腕だけでボールを上げてしまいます。これではコントロールができません。
21. ひざを十分に曲げて、前傾姿勢をとり、下半身ごとに伸びて、身体全体でボールを目的の場所におくるイメージでパスします。

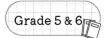
Ball Sports

Volleyball

Teacher

1 It doesn't have to be three times.

2 You can return the ball to the opponent's court on the first or second try, but then there might

3 be someone who cannot touch the ball.

4 So, in our grade, the rule is to return the ball after three passes.

5 First, let's start with the serve.

You hold the ball in your left hand, stand in front of the net, bend your legs and

6 crouch down.

7 That's right. Pull your right leg back.

8 Make a fist with your right hand, palm side facing up.

Lift the ball in your left hand to shoulder height and hit the bottom part of the ball as it falls,

9 scooping it with your right fist and wrist area, into the opponent's court.

10 Yes, very good.

11 Next is receiving.

12 With your arms outstretched, place both palms on top of each other with your palms facing up.

13 This will form a triangle from your shoulders to your hands.

14 Within this triangle, hit back the ball that just served and pass it to your teammates.

15 Please keep your body in a mid-rise position, with both feet parallel to each other.

16 We should receive the ball below your shoulder.

So, what does that mean we should do? When you are receiving the ball, it is important to firmly

17 extend your elbows and receive the ball with the triangle you made by both arms.

If your arms drop at this point, you will swing your arms when you catch the ball, and

18 not be able to control it.

19 The image is to hit the ball with your arms extended and the front of them being parallel.

If you move to the ball with your knees fully extended and standing up, your jaw will also be up.

20 You will only be able to raise the ball with your arms, and you will lose control of the ball.

It is important to bend your knees fully, lean forward, and use your entire body to visualize

21 where you want to send the ball as you pass.

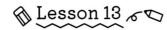
高学年

球技運動
バレーボール説明

先生

1. では、レシーブでキャッチボールをやってみましょう。3人一組になってください。
2. 2人が向い合せになって、一人はボール拾いを行います。
3. ボール拾いの担当からボールを投げてもらったら、レシーブして相手にパスします。
4. パスをレシーブしたら、相手に戻します。
5. ボールを落とさないで何回やれるか練習して下さい。
6. ボール拾いは、回数を数えてあげて、ボールが床に落ちたら拾って、また渡してやってください。
7. ボールを腕で跳ね上げてはダメですよ。遠くに飛んで行ってしまいます。
8. 伸ばした腕に当てて跳ね返すんですよ。
9. ボールの落ちてくるところに素早く移動して、正面でレシーブですよ。

10. では、次にトスを練習しましょう。
11. トスは、相手のコートにボールを打ち返せるように、ボールをアタックする人が打ちやすいところに上げるという動作です。
12. トスは、おでこのあたりに、両手の手の平を開いてハの字にして構えて、落ちてきたボールを上げるます。この時ボールを手で掴んではいけません。ボールを手のひらで受けて、上に押し出します。

13. では、トスの姿勢をして見て下さい。
14. 足を曲げて中腰になります。肘を方より上にセットします。肘が下がっていると、ボールが顔面に当たることになります。小野さんのメガネに当たっちゃいますからね。

15. では、ボールを上げますよ。トスして、先生の方に上げて見て下さい。
16. 違います。トスして、ボールを上にあげる瞬間に、膝を肘が両方伸びて、体ごと、ボールを押し上げるんです。そうです、そうです。
17. では、また、3人一組になって、一人はボールをあげて、一人は、もう一人のところにトスしてください。
18. 先ほどのレシーブと区別するためにトスと言って、練習していますが、このトスはアタックする人にボールを上げるためだけでなく、頭より高いところにボールが飛んできた場合のレシーブにもなります。
19. 腕で三角形を作ってボールを受けるのをアンダーレシーブ、トスのような格好でボールをうけるのをオーバーレシーブといいます。
20. では、オーバーレシーブでキャッチボールをしてみますよ。

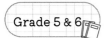
Grade 5 & 6

Ball Sports

1

Volleyball

Teacher

1. Now let's play catch in the receiving position. Please make groups of three.

2. Two people will face each other, with the third person in charge of picking up the ball.

3. When the ball is thrown to you, receive and pass the ball back to your opponent.

4. After receiving the pass, return the ball to your opponent.

5. Let's practice how many times you can do this without dropping the ball.

   For those who are in charge of picking up the ball, please count the number of times for each

6. rally, and when the ball falls to the floor, pick it up and start the counting over again.

7. Don't bounce the ball with your arm. It will fly far away.

8. You have to hit it with your outstretched arm and it will smoothly bounce back.

9. Move quickly to where the ball will fall and try to receive it in front of you.

10. Now let's practice tossing.

    Tossing is the action of raising the ball to a place where it is easier for the attacker to hit the ball

11. back into the opponent's court.

    When tossing, hold the palms of both of your hand's above forehead, with your index fingers

    and thumbs connected. Do not grab the ball with your hand at this point. Catch the ball with

12. your palms and push it upward.

13. Now, can you take a tossing stance

    Bend your knees and crouch down. Set your elbows above your shoulders. If your elbow is down,

14. the ball will hit you in the face. That means it will hit Ono-san's glasses, too.

15. Now, I will pass the ball. Toss it and pass it toward me.

    That's a little different. When you are tossing the ball, both knees and elbows should be

16. extended and you should use your whole body to push the ball up. That's right, good!

    Now, again, please make groups of three. One person throws the ball up in the air, the second

17. person should make a toss to the third person.

    We call it a toss to distinguish it from the receiving we just practiced. However, a toss can be

18. used to receive the ball if it flies above your head.

    When you make a triangle with your arms to receive the ball is called under-receiving while

19. receiving the ball in a toss-like position is called over-receiving.

20. Now, let's pass the ball back and forth using only over-receives.

P. E.

高学年

球技運動

バレーボールゲーム

先生

ゲームのルールを説明しますね。

まずは 3 人一チームとします。

ボールは一人 1 回触れて、3 人目の人が相手方のコートにボールを返せなかったら、

相手方が 1 点の得点、ボールを返せて相手方が同じように 3 人目の人が戻せなかったら、

自分の方が 1 点得点とします。

また、サーブがコートの外に飛び出した場合、打ち返すときにネットに触れた場合、

手と腕以外でボールを受けた場合はいずれも相手方の得点とします。

5 点最初に得点した方が勝ちとします。

それぞれのコートの真ん中に線が引いてありますね。この線の後ろからサーブをします。

レシーブをする人、トスをする人、相手のコートに返す人は、順番に代わります。

レシーブする人と、相手のコートに返す人はコート真ん中より後ろ、トスをする人は

コートよりネット寄りに立って下さい。

最初のサーブはじゃんけんで勝ったチームが行い、そのあとは得点したチームが

サーブすることにします。

ルールはわかりましたか。

要は、一人 1 回、チームで 3 回目に相手方のコートに返すことで、

床に落としたら相手の得点になりますから、協力して、次の人が打ちやすい場所と高さを

考えてボールを繋いでいきます。

Lesson 13

Ball Sports

Grade 5 & 6

Volleyball Game

Teacher

1 Let me explain the rules of the game.

2 First of all, we will have teams of three players.

3 Each person should touch the ball once, and if the third person fails to return the ball to the opponent's court, the opponent scores one point. Similarly, if the third person returns the ball and the opponent fails to do the same, you score one point.

4 In addition, if the ball goes out of the court, touches the net when hitting back, or if the ball is received with anything other than the hands and arms, the opponent scores a point.

5 The first team to score 5 points wins.

6 Do you see a line drawn in the middle of each court. You serve from behind this line.

7 The person who receives the ball, tosses it, and returns it to the opponent's court is rotated.

8 The receiver and the person who returns the ball to the opponent's court should stand behind the middle of the court, and the person who tosses the ball should stand closer to the net.

9 The first serve will be made by the team that wins rock-paper-scissors. After that, the team that just scored will serve.

10 Do you understand the rules?

The main point is that each person in the team must touch the ball once and return it to the opponent's court by the third pass, and if it drops to the floor, the opponent scores.

11 Working together, pass the ball to the next person at the right place and height so they can easily hit it.

運動会の準備

低学年

予行練習

先生

1 運動会が近づいてきました。

2 今日は、予行練習をします。

3 他のクラスと一緒に練習しますから、行儀よくしてください。

4 では、まず行進と整列の練習をします。

5 先生の笛の合図で、進めます。

6 全員気をつけ！ピー！

7 各組2列に整列！ピー！

8 右腕を腰！肘が隣に当たらないように。横に広がれ！

9 ピー！

10 体は正面のまま、顔だけ左向け左！

11 左を見て、横一列を作れ！

12 前向け前！では、音楽を合わせて、その場で行進始め！ピ！ピ！ピ！

13 右、左、右、左。腕を振って。腕は、足と逆ですよ。

14 ちょっと、そこ、足と腕が同じになっていますよ。気を付けて。

15 下を向かないで。顔を上げて、前を見て！

16 では、前へ進め！　列を崩さない！右、左、右、左！

17 全体止まれ！前を向いて！並んで！広がれ！

18 皆さん、よくできました。先生の指示にもっと従うと、お客様からも、とてもきれいに

19 見えます。この調子です。

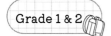

体育

P.E.

Grade 1 & 2

Preparing for Sports Day

Practice Session

Teacher

1 Sports day is coming soon.

2 So, from today we will start to practice.

3 We are going to practice with other classes so I want you to behave well.

4 First, we are going to practice marching.

5 When I blow my whistle, start.

6 Everyone, stand up straight! (Beep!)

7 Each group stand in two rows. (Beep!)

8 Put your right arm on your hip. Spread out! Be careful so your elbow doesn't touch others.

7 (Beep!)

10 Look to your left while your body faces front.

11 Look to your left and make one horizontal line.

12 Face forward! March with the music. Start marching. (Beep! Beep! Beep!)

130 Right-left, right-left. Swing your arms. Your arms swing in the opposite direction of your legs.

14 Don't swing your arms and legs in the same direction at the same time.

15 Don't look down. Look up, look forward!

16 Alright, move forward. Keep a straight line. Right, left, right, left!

17 Everyone, stop! Face forward! Line up. Spread out!

18 Well done everyone. The better you listen to my orders, the better it looks from the audience's

19 view. Keep up the good work. OK,

Lesson 14 体育 / P.E.

高学年

運動会の準備 2
棒倒しと騎馬戦の説明

先生 📢

1. 棒倒しは男子だけで行い、騎馬戦は男女一緒に行います。

2. 棒倒しは男子だけの種目ですが、説明はみんなに聞いてもらいますね。

3. 棒倒しは、相手方の棒を倒すか棒のてっぺんの旗を取れば勝ちです。

4. 赤組、白組それぞれが攻撃メンバーと守備メンバーに分かれて、攻撃メンバーは相手方の守備メンバーの守る棒に向かって攻撃します。

5. 守備メンバーは相手方の攻撃メンバーから棒を守ります。

6. 参加者は全員、上半身裸、はだしです。

7. これはシャツを引っ張って倒したり、運動靴で蹴ったりしてケガをしないようにするためです。

8. 1年生のときから上級生の棒倒しを見てきたので、わかっていると思いますが、げんこつで叩いたり、足で蹴ったりしてはいけません。

9. 攻撃メンバーと守備メンバーは身長で大体決まります。

10. 棒倒しの予行練習は、全体練習の時に一度行います。

先生 📢

1. では、次に騎馬戦の説明をします。

2. 騎馬戦は、4人一組になり、3人が騎馬になり、一人が上に乗って、相手の騎馬の上に乗っている人から帽子を取ると勝ちとなり、赤組、白組で勝った議場の多い方が勝ちとなります。

3. 騎馬戦のチームは騎馬になる人については大体同じ身長の人で組みます。

4. 身長差があると、騎馬がどちらかに傾くことになるからです。

5. 上に乗る人は、身長が低い人か体重の軽い人です。

6. 重いと騎馬が持ちません。

7. 騎馬戦の前に、赤組、白組それぞれでどのように戦うか作戦を立てます。

8. この作戦がかなり重要です。

9. 5年生の女子の騎馬と、6年生の男子の騎馬が戦えば6年生の男子の騎馬が勝ってしまいます。

10. ですが6年生男子の騎馬を残しておくと、仲間の騎馬の帽子を次々に取られます。だから、真っ先に3騎馬が一斉に6年生男子騎馬を負かしてしまうといった作戦を立てます。

11. 騎馬のチームはもうすぐ決まるので、決まったら昼休みや放課後に騎馬を組んで走る練習をします。そうしないと、当日にうまく走れなかったり、騎馬が崩れて失格になったりします。

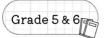 **Lesson 14**

Preparing for Sports Day

Pole Toppling and Cavalry Battle

Grade 5 & 6

Teacher

1. The pole toppling is for boys only, and the cavalry battle is for both boys and girls together.

2. As I said the pole toppling is for boys only, but I want everyone listen to the explanation.

In pole toppling, the winner is the one who knocks down the opponent's pole or captures

3. the flag at the top of the pole.

The red and white teams are divided into offense and defense team. The offense team should

4. attack the stick guarded by the defending members of the opponent.

5. The defending members should protect their sticks from the offense members of the other team.

6. All participants are barefoot and shirtless.

This is to prevent somebody from pulling on your shirt to bring you down or from someone

7. kicking you and injuring you with their shoes.

You have been watching this since you were in the first grade so I'm sure you understand

8. the basics. You must not hit anyone with your fists or kick them with your feet.

9. Attacking and defending members are generally determined by height.

10. The pole toppling practice will be done when we have the whole school rehearsal.

Teacher

1. Next, I will explain the cavalry battle.

In the cavalry battle, four people form a team, three of them form a horse, and one rides on

2. top of the others. The winner is the one who takes the hat off the rider on the other team's horse.

3. In the cavalry battle, teams are usually made up of people of the same height as the rider.

4. This is because a difference in height will cause the riders to lean to one side or the other.

5. The person who rides on top should be shorter or lighter in weight.

6. If the rider is heavy, the horse will not be able to hold the rider.

Before the cavalry battle, the red and white teams must strategize

7. and plan how they will fight each other.

8. This strategy is quite important.

If we allow the 5th grade girls' cavalry and the 6th grade boys' cavalry to fight, the 6th grade

9. boys' cavalry will most likely win.

However, if you leave the 6th grade boys' cavalry until the end, you can take the hats of other

cavalries one after the another. So, the strategy here is to have the three cavalries come together

10. to defeat the 6th grade boys' cavalry.

The cavalry teams will be decided soon, so once they are decided, we will practice riding in teams

during lunch break and after school. If you don't, you may not be able to run well on the day of

11. the competition, or your horse may collapse and you will be disqualified.

Lesson 14

体育

P.E.

高学年

運動会の準備

リハーサル

先生

1. 今日は運動会の予行練習を行います。予行練習だからといって、気を緩めることなく真剣にやってください。まず、騎馬戦の予行練習をおこないます。

2. では、入場してきて、赤組、白組それぞれの組に分かれてください。

3. 今から騎馬戦をやります。ルールを説明します。

4. ・試合時間はおよそ３分です。

5. ・帽子はうしろかぶりしなさい。ゴムひもはかけないでください。

6. ・体当たりは良いですが、騎馬が相手の騎馬を蹴ったりしてはいけません。

7. ・帽子を取ったら、グランドに捨てて構いません。

8. ・帽子を取られた騎馬はすぐに騎馬を解いて陣地に戻ってください。

9. ・試合が終わって陣地に帰るまでに騎馬が崩れたら失格です。

10. １回戦はたくさんの騎馬が残った方が勝ちとします。
同じ数だった場合は、大将騎馬の一騎打ちとします。２回戦は大将を守って最後まで

11. 大将が生き残っていたほうが勝ちとします。

12. では、１回戦を始めます。騎馬を作れ。

13. よーい、バン。　ヤメ　パンッ（号砲）　もどりなさい

14. 騎馬を数えます　１、２、３、・・・ ただいまの勝負、赤組の勝ち！！

15. 帽子を拾いなさい。陣地を交代して、２回戦を行います。

16. ２回戦を行います　大将を倒したら勝ちです。

17. 騎馬を作れ。用意　バンッ（号砲）

18. ヤメ　バンッ（号砲）　もどりなさい

19. ただいまの勝負、白の勝ち！！「帽子を拾いなさい」

20. あいさつ、　ありがとうございました

21. 退場します。退場したら、朝礼台の前に戻ってきて整列して下さい。

22. はい、お疲れ様でした。きびきびしていてよかったと思います。

23. ただ、始まった途端に騎馬が崩れるチームがありました。

24. 騎馬の手がきちんとつながっていなかったようです。
騎馬の先頭と左右の人との手のつなぎ方は指と指を絡めて、しっかりと繋いでください。

25. また、左右の人は出来るだけ近づいて、上の人は左右の人の肩の上に座るようにして、

26. 戦うときだけ立ちあがってください。

27. 立ちあがったままでいると、騎馬の人の腕が疲れて離れてしまいます。

 **Lesson 14**

P.E.

Grade 5 & 6

 **Preparing for Sports Day** 3

Rehearsal

Teacher

Today we will practice for the Sports Day. Please do not relax just because it is a rehearsal,

1 but please take it seriously. First, we will practice the cavalry battle.

2 Now, please come in and divide into your red and white teams.

3 Now we will start the cavalry battle. I will explain the rules.

4 •The duration of the game is approximately 3 minutes.

5 •Your hats must be worn backwards. Do not wear a rubber band.

6 •You may hit the opponent's horse, but you may not kick the opponent's horse.

7 •If a rider takes off an opponent's hat, he may simply throw it on the ground.

8 •Any rider whose hat is taken should immediately dismount and return to your base.

•After the game, if your cavalry collapses before you reach your team's base position,

9 you are disqualified.

10 In the first round, the team with the most cavalry remaining wins.

If it is a tie, the winner will be determined by a one-to-one fight between the captains of the

11 cavalries. In the second round, the team that can protect their captain the longest is the winner.

12 Now, let's begin the first round. Please build your cavalry.

13 Ready! (Bang!) Stop! (Bang!) Go back!

14 Count the riders. One, two, three..... The red team wins!

15 Please pick up your hats. Let's switch sides and play a second round.

16 Let's start the second round. Remember, If you take down the general, you win.

17 Now make your cavalry. Ready, (bang!)

18 Stop! (Bang!) Go back!

19 The white team wins the game! Please pick up your hats.

20 Greet each other and say thank you.

It's time to leave. Before you leave, please come back and line up in front of the morning

21 assembly table.

22 Yes, thank you very much for your hard work. I think it was good that you were so prompt.

23 However, there was a team whose cavalry collapsed as soon as they started.

24 It seems that the riders' hands were not connected properly.

Please make sure that the hands of the leader of the cavalry and the people on the left and

25 right are firmly connected by interlacing your fingers.

Also, the people on the left and right should be as close as possible, with the leader sitting on

26 the shoulders of the people on the left and right, and should only stand up when fighting.

27 If they remain standing up, the arms of the person on the horse will get tired and separate.

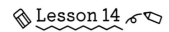

体育

P.E.

運動会

運動会の起源はヨーロッパですが、日本の運動会のように、参加者が一定のプログラムについて全体としてまとまりながら競技・演技を行う形式の体育的行事は、日本独特の体育的行事です。運動会が日本で行われだしたのは明治時代で、最初に行われた運動会は、定説によれば 1874 年 3 月 21 日、海軍兵学寮で行われた競闘遊戯会であるとされ、イギリス人英語教師フレデリック・ウィリアム・ストレンジさんの指導によって行われました。

この日本独特の運動会を英語で簡単に説明してみましょう。

At schools, children practice for and participate in their school's undokai, a Sports Day. They have all kinds of events, and will sometimes practice for weeks in advance.

Elementary school students enjoyed games such as a big ball relay and bean bag toss. It normally takes place on the school's fields.

運動会の種目を説明してみましょう。

大玉送り (Big Ball Relay)

2-4 チームに分かれ、チームごとに色の違う大玉を手を使い頭の上で前から後ろに送ります。後ろの人が早く前の人に持ってきたチームが勝利となります。

Students are divided into teams (two-four) and are given a giant ball (the color differs depending on their team), which they have to push with their hands above their heads, starting from the front line to the back, then to the front again in the quickest possible time.

玉いれ (Bean Bag Toss)

玉入れは幼児から高齢者までが楽しめる競技の一つで、小豆は大豆等を布で覆われた「玉」(お手玉)を高い位置にあるカゴに、どれだけ、決められた時間内に入れることができるかを競います。

Tama ire (ball-toss game) requires speed and accuracy. It is a game where balls (usually made of cloth) are thrown into a basket on a high pole within a specified time. The team that has more balls in the basket wins.

音楽
subject 7
Music

Lesson 01

音楽

Music

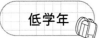 低学年

楽しく歌おう

先生

1. 音楽の時間ですから、音楽を使っていろんなことをやってみましょう。
2. 「ドレミファソ」と弾いたら、立って先生の方を向いてください。
3. 「ドミソ」の和音を弾いたら、挨拶をします。
4. 「ソファミレド」と弾いたら、座ってください。
5. 分かりましたか。
6. では、「ドレミファソ」。
7. 「ドミソ」。
8. 「ソファミレド」。
9. はい、よくできました。

10. では、次に、この曲を先生が弾いたら、その場で足踏みをします。
11. 「きらきら星」という曲です。
12. そうです、皆さん上手ですね。トン、トン、トン、トン、トン、トン、
13. トン、トン、トン、休み、トン、トン・・・・

14. では、きらきら星のリズムで、教室を行進してみましょう。
15. 歌を歌いながら、行進してみます。
16. 皆さん、教室の壁のところに、移動してください。いいですか、移動したら、まず、
17. 教室の真ん中を向いてください。

18. はい、全員、右側を体ごと向いてください。
19. では、まずは、その場で足踏み、先生が『ハイ』と言ったら、行進しますよ。
20. そして、もう一度、『はい』と言ったら、その場で足踏みします。
21. ♪ドドソソララソ
22. はい
23. ♪ファファミミレレド
24. はい
25. ♪ソソファファミミレ

26. はい、よくできました。
27. 自分の席に戻って、「ソファミレド」。

Lesson 01

音楽

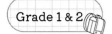

Grade 1 & 2

Let's Enjoy Singing

Teacher

1. This is music class, so we will enjoy this time using music.

2. Ok, so if you hear ♪ C, D, E, F, G, please face towards me.

3. If you hear ♪ C, D, E then stand up and say hi to me.

4. And if you hear ♪ G, F, E, D, C, please sit down.

5. Understood?

6. Ok so, (on organ: ♪ C, D, E, F, G)

7. ♪ (C, D, E)

8. ♪ (G, F, E, D, C)

9. Well done!

10. Next, I want you to stamp your feet to the song.

11. ♪ (play Twinkle, Twinkle Little Star)

12. Great, everyone! (Stamp, stamp, stamp, stamp...)

13. One, two, three rest, one, two, three, rest

14. OK, now let's start marching around the classroom to this rhythm.

15. We'll march as we sing.

16. Everyone, I want you to move next to the wall.

17. OK, now I want you to face towards the middle of the classroom.

18. Now, turn right.

18. Next, make some steps where you are at now. Once I say "hai," start marching.

20. Another "hai" will be the signal to stop.

21. ♪ Twinkle, twinkle little star

22. (Hai)

23. ♪ How I wonder what you are

24. (Hai)

25. ♪ Up above the world so high

26. Looks good!

27. Now go back to your seat. ♪ (G, F, E, D, C)

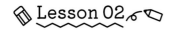
音階

先生

1 もっと、上手になりたいと思いませんか。

2 そのためには、音楽のいろんなルールを知ることが必要です。

3 ルールをいろいろ覚えていきましょう。

4 まず、行進で弾いたきらきら星を、先生が、黒板にかいたカタカナで、歌いましょう。

5 ドドソソララソ　ファファミミレレド

6 ソソファファミミレ　ソソファファミミレ

7 ドドソソララソ　ファファミミレレド

8 使ったカタカナを○で囲みました。

9 これを、低い音から順に並べますよ。

10 オルガンで音を出しながら行いますから、音も聞いてください。

11 はい、音を聞いても分かりましたね。

12 ド、レ、ミ、ファ、ソ、ラの順です。

13 これにラの後ろに、シ、ドを加えると、ドレミファソラシドとなります。

14 これで、皆さんが、ますます上手に歌うための基本の一つを、知りましたね。

15 これを音階といって、どの歌も、この音階の組み合わせで、曲が作られています。

16 では、きらきら星の曲を見てみましょうね。

17 これを楽譜といいます。

18 では、この楽譜を見ながら、みんなで歌ってみましょう。

19 次の授業から、鍵盤ハーモニカを使いますから、忘れずに持ってきてくださいね。

Lesson 02

音楽

The Musical Scale

Grade 1 & 2

Teacher

1 Do you want to learn to play the organ like this or another kind of instrument?

2 In order to learn how to play an instrument, there are a few rules we need to follow.

3 Try to remember the rules.

4 First, you need to sing the notes to Twinkle, Twinkle Little Star. I have written it on the board.

5 C, C, G, G, A, A, G   F, F, E, E, D, D, C

6 G, G, F, F, E, E, D   G, G, F, F, E, E, D

7 C, C, G, G, A, A, G,   F, F, E, E, D, D, C

8 I've circled the katakana we use for this.

9 This starts at a low note.

10 Listen to me play the notes on the organ and listen for the difference.

11 Here we go, in order.

12 C, D, E, F, G, A.

13 After A, we go to B and then back to C again.

14 With this basic rule, now you are on your way to becoming even better singers.

15 This is called a musical scale. All songs are made with these notes.

16 So, let's look at Twinkle, Twinkle Little Star.

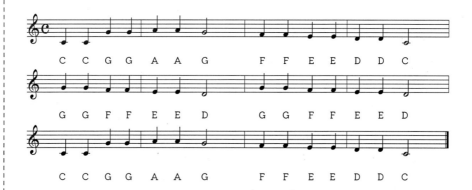

17 This is called a sheet music.

18 Now, let's sing the song together while looking at this sheet music.

19 From the next lesson, we will be using the keyboard harmonica (melodica), so don't forget to bring it with you.

音楽

楽器
鍵盤ハーモニカ

先生

1 鍵盤ハーモニカを出してください。

2 では、今日から、この鍵盤ハーモニカが弾けるように練習します。

3 まず、机の上に、黒色の吹き口部分を左にして、鍵盤ハーモニカを置いてください。

4 白い鍵盤と少し高くなっている黒い鍵盤があります。

5 いまから、皆さんにシールを配りますから、左から5番目の白い鍵盤に、シールを貼ってください。

6 この鍵盤が、「ド」という音です。

7 音階は、この「ド」という音から始まります。

8 そして、白い鍵盤は、順番に「ドレミファソラシド」と、音が、少しずつ高くなるようになっています。

9 黒板を見てください。

10 「ドレミファソラシド」は、音が8個ありますね。

11 指は5本ですね。3個分の指が足りませんね。だから、途中で、指を繰り返し使わないと、弾けませんね。

12 黒板を見てください。

13 黒板の鍵盤ハーモニカの絵の鍵盤を、先生が、指で押してみますよ。「ド、レ、ミ」、ここで、親指を「ファ」のキーに持ってきて、「ファ、ソ、ラ、シ、ド」。

14 最後の「ド」は小指ですね。

先生

1 では、先生が音階を歌いますから、皆さんは音階の鍵盤キーを押さえる練習しましょう。

2 押さえることができるようになりましたか。

3 では、実際に音を出してみましょうね。

4 まず、左手で、鍵盤ハーモニカを口のそばまで持ち上げて、目で見えるようにしてください。

5 先生を見てください。このような感じです。はい、やってみてください。

6 そしたら、吹き口をくわえて、前歯で挟んで、口を閉じてください。

7 では、フッと息を吹き出してください。

8 息を吹きながら、鍵盤のドを押してください。

9 はい、そうです。

10 そして、吹きながら、鍵盤を押したり、指を離したりしてください。

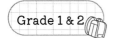

音楽

Musical Instruments 1

Melodicas

Grade 1 & 2

Teacher

1. OK everyone, please take out your melodicas.

2. From today, we are going to start practicing the melodica.

3. First off, place your melodica with the black part on the left. The black part is where you will be blowing in air as you play.

4. And, you see, there are black keys and white keys on the keyboard. Their height is different too.

5. I am going to give you a sticker and I want you to stick it on the fifth key from the left.

6. That's the key for the C note.

7. This is the basic starting point in music.

8. And then, we have C, D, E, F, G, A, B, C on the white keys. Notice that the sound becomes higher.

9. Look at the board, everyone.

10. There are 8 notes in the scale, right?

11. But we only have five fingers. This means that we have to play 3 keys somehow without extra fingers. We need to move our hand and reuse fingers.

12. Please look at the blackboard.

13. I am going to press the keys on the melodica.

14. C, D, E like this, and then, for F, you are going to shift your thumb, and then the last C will be pressed with your fifth finger.

Teacher

1. Next, I am going to sing, but you are going to practice pressing the keys on the melodica.

2. Is everyone okay now?

3. Now we are going to actually make some sound with it.

4. First, use your left hand to hold the melodica and bring it near your mouth. It should be high enough so you can see the keys you are playing.

5. Look at how I'm doing it. It's like this. Now everyone please try it.

6. Now, put the black mouthpiece into your mouth, gently biting it with your front teeth.

7. You should also close your mouth around it. Then, blow some air from your lungs.

8. While you are blowing it, press the C key.

9. Exactly, that's right guys!

10. Practice a few times to make some sounds with your melodica.

低学年

楽器
カスタネット

先生

1. この楽器は、分かりますか。
2. カスタネットです。
3. カスタネットは、2枚の板をたたいて、音を出す楽器です。
4. 掌にのる、とても小さな楽器ですが、大きな音がでます。
5. カスタネットは、ピアノと違い、音が一つしか出ません。
6. だから、強さを変えたり、スピードを変えて打ちます。

7. では、持ち方ですが、赤い方を下にして、左手の人差し指にゴムの輪を通して、赤い方を下にして、手のひらに置き、軽く包むようにして持ってください。
8. はい、左手の掌を上向きにして、右手の指をそろえて、指先で軽く打ちます。

低学年

楽器
小太鼓

先生

1. これは、知っていますか
2. 小太鼓は、カスタネットと同じように一つの音を出す打楽器です。
3. それで、リズムを演奏するのに使います。
4. 小太鼓は、胴に皮が張ってあり、張ってある皮の部分をバチで叩いて音を出します。
5. バチの持ち方は、こうです。
6. 右手と左手で、柄の下から三分の一くらいのところを持ちます。
7. 親指をばちの柄の上にのせ、残りの指で、軽く握ります。
8. 小太鼓は、たたく場所によって、少し音が違います。

9. きらきら星を小太鼓のリズムで、歌ってみましょう。
10. では、順番に、小太鼓を叩いてみましょう。
11. 注意ですが、小太鼓の高さは人によって調整します。
12. だいたい、お腹の高さです。

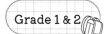
Grade 1 & 2

Musical Instruments
Castanets

Teacher

1. Does anyone know what these are?
2. These are castanets.
3. Castanets are instruments that are made by striking two boards to produce sound.
4. They are small enough to fit in your palm, but make a big sound.
5. Castanets, unlike the piano, are an instrument with only one tone.
6. So, you can hit them soft or hard. Fast or slow.
7. The way to hold it is to keep the red side on your palm and your index finger should go through the loop. The rest of your fingers should cover up the instrument easily.
8. You should hold them with your left hand, by the way. Then use the fingers on your right-hand to lightly hit the blue side.

Grade 1 & 2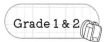

Musical Instruments
Small Drums

Teacher

1. Everyone, do you know what this is?
2. Like the castanets, small drums are also a type of percussion which only makes one tone.
3. So, we use it to play rhythm.
4. You hit the head of the drum, which is made of thin leather.
5. This is how you hold the sticks.
6. Hold them for each hand around one third up from the bottom.
7. Hold the stick firmly with your thumb and lightly hold it with rest of your fingers.
8. Actually, the sound that the small drum makes is different depending on where you hit it.
9. Now let's sing and play Twinkle, Twinkle Little Star with the drum.
10. Let's take turns playing it now.
11. One caution though, each person should adjust the height of the drum for yourself.
12. It should be about the height of your stomach.

 低学年

リズム
音符

先生

音楽は、歌ったときにわかるように、音の高さと低さ、これを音階といい、音の長さ、これを音符といい、これらで表現されています。

きらきら星で、みんなが歌った、「ドドソソララソ」で、音の高低がありましたね。

黒板を見てください。

代表的な音符は4つです。

ぼう　はた　たま

全音符　　2分音符　　4分音符　　8分音符

連こう

音符のそれぞれの部分には名前があって、たま、ぼう、はたと言います。

一番使うのは、4分音符です。

全音符は、4分音符の4つ分の長さです。2分音符は、4分音符の2つ分、8分音符は、4分音符の半分の長さです。

きらきら星の楽譜を見てください。4分音符で歌い、2小節目に2分音符があって、そこだけ長く伸ばしますね。

楽譜の一番前にある記号は、ト音記号といって、この楽譜は、右手用の楽譜であることを示しています。

まだ、鍵盤ハーモニカを右手だけで弾いていますが、次第に上手になると、オルガンもピアノも、両手で弾けるようになります。

左手用の楽譜ですよーという記号は、ヘ音記号といいます。

ドドソソララソ　ファファミミレレド
ソソファファミミレ　ソソファファミミレ
ドドソソララソ　ファファミミレレド

ト音記号　　ヘ音記号

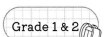 Lesson 04

音楽

Music

Grade 1 & 2

Rhythm
Tones

Teacher

As you know from singing, there are high and low sounds. These sounds are called tones in music. We can express the length of sounds using notes.

And we also had some different tones when we sang Twinkle, Twinkle Little Star.

Now, please look at the blackboard.

There are four main types of notes.

Stem   Flag

Notehead

Beam

A whole note   half note   quarter note   eighth note

Each part of the note has a name too, like the head, the stem, and the flag.

Quarter notes are used quite often.

A whole note is the length of a four quarter notes, a half note is two quarter notes and eighth note is half of a quarter note.

Now, please look at the notes of the song. We mostly sing using quarter notes but there are some half notes where we stretch the sound.

What you see at the very beginning of the score is called the treble clef.

This tells you that you are supposed to use your right hand.

So far, we have only used our right hand to play, but as we improve you will start to use your left hand too.

There is also the bass clef which is mostly used for lower notes.

C C G G A A G   F F E E D D C

G G F F E E D   G G F F E E D

C C G G A A G   F F E E D D C

Treble Clef   Bass Clef

低学年

リズム
休符と指くぐり

先生 📢

知っておかないといけないのは、音を出さない休符という記号です。

休符を付けると、タン、タン、休み、タン、タン、休み等、音を出さないところを作ることができ、広がりがでます。

休符は、音符に合わせて、全休符、2分休符、4分休符、8分休符があり、

| 全休 | 2分休符 | 4分休符 | 8休符 |

と表します。

では、鍵盤ハーモニカで一曲弾いてみましょう。

音符の下の数字は、右手5本の指の番号です。

親指が1、人差し指が2、中指が3、薬指が4、小指が5です。

指くぐりのやり方を説明します。

指くぐり

1 2 3 1 2 3 4 5

「ド・レ・ミ」と弾いたら親指（1の指）を「ファ」からは普通に親指（1の指）から順に弾いていきます。

親指をほかの指の下からくぐらせて、「ファ」の鍵盤の上にもっていきます。

練習をして、上手にできるようになったら、低いドから高いドまで、指くぐりをして弾いてみましょう。

これで、音が切れずに、なめらかにメロディーを弾くことができます。

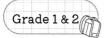
Grade 1 & 2

Rhythm
Rest Note

Teacher

Another thing you must remember is the rest note which does not produce a sound.

You need to pause at this symbol.

For example, with this, you can make a rhythm like, "One, two, rest, one, two, rest."

It gives the music a wider range.

There are different kinds of rest notes as well, which match the main types of notes:

a whole rest   half rest   quarter rest   eighth rest.

Now let's actually play a song.

The numbers below the notes are the numbers of the five fingers of the right hand.

1 for the thumb, 2 for the index finger, 3 for the middle finger,

4 for the ring finger, and 5 for the little finger.

Here is an explanation of the fingering technique

Fingering Technique

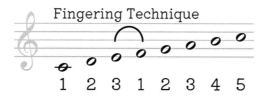

1   2   3   1   2   3   4   5

When playing C, D, E start with your thumb and then move your thumb over to play F.

Place your thumb under the other fingers and place it on the "F" keyboard. Move your hand up the keys.

With a little practice you will get better, let's play the scale from C to C.

We want to play this smoothly without any breaks in between.

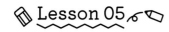

音楽

拍子

低学年

先生

1 黒板に注目。楽譜を貼っています。

2 この楽譜をみると、まず、ト音記号になっていますから、右手用の楽譜をわかります。

3 次に、4/4と書いてあるのは、区切り目これを小節といい、1小節に4分音符が4個入る拍子になっているということを指し、この曲は4拍子の曲となります。

4 2小節目と4小節目は、音符が3つしかありませんね。

でも、最後の音符が2分音符になっていますから、4分音符が2つ分ですから、

5 4分音符4つと同じです。

6 2段目の3小節目は、8つの音符があり、二つずつ、音符が繋がっています。

7 4分音符の半分の8分音符が8つありますから、4分音符4つと同じです。

8 ですから、手拍子をつけるときは、パンパンパンパンの4回手を叩くか、2小節目では、パンパンパーンと最後の手拍子の長さを2回分伸ばします。

9 黒板を見てください。この曲は、3分の4の曲、つまり、3拍子の曲です。

10 手拍子を付けて歌って、確認しましょう。

こいのぼり

Carp Streamer

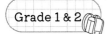

音楽

Beat

Teacher

1 Please look at the blackboard. Here is the score.

2 Looking at this, we see that the first sign is a treble clef, meaning you should use your right hand.

Next, it says 4/4, which is the dividing line, and this is called a measure, which means that there

3 are four quarter notes in one measure. This also means that the song is a 4-beat song, too.

4 In the second and fourth bars, there are only three notes.

5 But the last note is a half note so it is two quarter notes, which is the same as four quarter notes.

6 The third measure of the second row has eight notes, two of which are connected to each other.

There are eight eighth notes, half of a quarter note, so it is the same as four quarter notes.

Also, the 3rd part of the second row also has a different symbol, right? This means that each of

7 them is eighth notes.

Therefore, when clapping, clap your hands four times with pan-pan-pan-pan or, in the second

8 measure, extend the length of the last clap by two times with pan-pan-pan-pan.

9 Please look at the blackboard. This song is in 3/4 time, meaning a 3-beat song.

10 Let's practice first by clapping.

こいのぼり

Carp Streamer

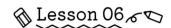
中学年

リコーダーをまなぶ

1

基礎

先生

1 今日からリコーダーの練習をします。

2 まずは、正しい姿勢と持ち方を身につけてください。

3 リコーダーの持ち方ですが、

4 腕や肩の力は抜いて口と右手親指でしっかり支えます。

5 リコーダーは 45 度くらいの角度に持ち、前方を見ます。

6 背筋はまっすぐ伸ばして構えます。

7 はい、構えてみてください。

8 右手と左手が反対になっていたり、肘が机についていたり、口の中に入れすぎている人はいませんか。

9 リコーダーを吹くにあたっては、タンギングに気を付けて吹きます。

10 まだ、音を出してはいけませんよ。

11 タンギングは、基本的には「トゥ」というように吹きます。

12 タンギングをせず大きくため息をつくように「フー」と息を入れたのでは、しっかりした表情のある音は出ません。

13 舌で息の出始めをコントロールすることが基本です。わかりましたね。

14 口に当てて、息を入れる部分を「吹き口」といいます

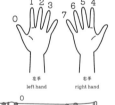

15 では、まずリコーダーの穴を押えることを覚えますよ。

16 指穴に番号をつけます。上から順に、1．2．3．…で一番下が 7 です。

17 後ろの穴は、0 です。指にも番号をつけます。

18 左手の親指が 0、人差し指が 1、中指が 2、薬指が 3 です。

19 右手は、人差し指が 4、中指が 5、薬指が 6、小指が 7 です。

20 1 〜 7 の指では、指先のふくらんだ所で穴をふさぎます。

21 でも、0 の指だけは、指の左斜め上の方で穴をふさぎます。

22 穴の位置が分かったら、指にギュッと力を入れてください。

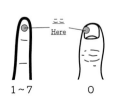

23 リコーダーを吹く時は、顔のどこにも力を入れないで、吹き口を下唇にちょこっと乗せるようなつもりで吹きます。

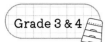 **Lesson 06**

Learning to play a Recorder 1

Basic

Teacher

1. Today we will start practicing the recorder.
2. First of all, we need to learn the correct posture and how to hold it.
3. So let me explain how to hold the recorder first.
4. Relax your arms and shoulders and hold the recorder firmly with your mouth and right thumb.
5. Hold the recorder at an angle of about 45 degrees and look forward.
6. Hold the recorder with your back straight.

7. Yes, try to hold the position.

Do you have your right and left hands opposite each other, your elbows on the desk,
8. or too much of the recorder in your mouth?

9. When playing the recorder, please be aware of your tongue.
10. Don't make a sound yet.
11. Tonguing is basically blowing a "toe" sound.

If you do not do tonguing and you blow with a "whoosh" as if you were breathing, you
12. will not be able to produce a firm, expressive sound.

The basic principle is to control the beginning of the breath with the tongue. Now, do you
13. understand?
14. The part that is placed against the mouth and breathed into is called the "mouthpiece".

15. Now, let's start with learning to hold the holes of the recorder.
16. Let's number the finger holes. From the top, 1...2...3...and the bottom is 7.
17. The back hole is 0. Fingers are also numbered as below.

On the left hand, the thumb is 0, the index finger is 1,
18. the middle finger is 2, and the ring finger is 3.

On the right hand, the index finger is 4, the middle finger is 5, the ring finger is 6, and the little
19. finger is 7.
20. On fingers 1 through 7, the holes are blocked with the fingertips.
21. But only for the 0 finger, the hole is blocked with the upper left diagonal of the finger.
22. When you find the position of the hole, squeeze your fingers together.

When you play the recorder, do not put pressure anywhere on your face,
23. but blow as if you were placing the mouth of the recorder on your lower lip.

中学年　　リコーダーをまなぶ　2
楽譜

先生 📢

では、楽譜を見てみましょう。

はい、この楽譜を見て、いくつが確認をしましょう。

この曲は、何拍子の曲ですか。

それはどういうことでしょうか。

各小節を見てみると、4分音符が4つ、4分音符が3つと4分休符、

それと最後の小節は付点2分音符です。4分音符3つと同じです。

だから、最後の小節は、トゥーゥーゥーと伸ばします。

4拍子というのは、ト音記号の横に 4/4 と書いてあるので分かりますね。

3/4 と書いてあれば、3拍子、2/4 と書いてあれば、2拍子の曲でしたね。

先生 📢

さて、楽譜の最初を見てください。ト音記号ですね。

この曲はト音記号なのに、リコーダーを吹くときに左手用のヘ音記号の楽譜がありませんね。

その理由は、ト音記号の楽譜を右手と左手の両方の指を使って押さえていますね。

だから、管楽器の楽譜はト音記号だけです。

楽譜の説明をしておきます。

1段目と2段目の最初のかっこのようなマークを中括弧といい、同時に演奏する段であることを示しています。

3段目と4段目の最後の2重の縦線は終止線といい、この曲はこれで終わりを示します。

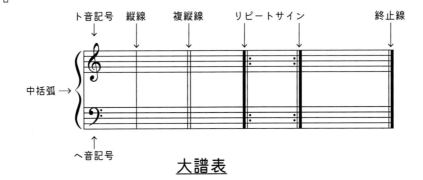

大譜表

Grade 3 & 4

Learning to play the Recorder 2

Music Score

Teacher
📢

1. Now, let's look at the music score.

2. Yes, let's go over some points after looking at this music score.

3. How many beats does this piece of music have?

4. And, what does that mean?

   If you look at each measure, there are four quarter notes, three quarter notes and a quarter rest,

5. and the last measure is a dotted half note, the same as three quarter notes.

6. So, you need to str……. etch the last bar.

7. You know it is 4 beats because it says 4/4 next to the G clef.

8. If it says 3/4, then it is a 3 beats song, and if it says 2/4, it is a 2 beats song.

Teacher
📢

1. Now, look at the beginning part of the score. This is a G clef, isn't it?

2. This piece has G clef, yet there is no F clef score for the left hand when playing the recorder.

3. That's why, you should hold the G clef with the fingers of both your right and left hands.

4. Therefore, the wind instrument score has only G clef.

5. Let me explain about the score then.

   The first bracketed mark in the first and second steps is called the brace, indicating that

6. they are the steps to be played at the same time.

   The double vertical line at the end of the third and fourth staves is called the end line and

7. indicates that this is the end of the piece.

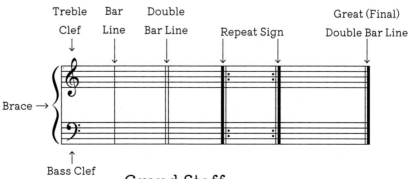

Treble Clef	Bar Line	Double Bar Line	Repeat Sign	Great (Final) Double Bar Line

Brace →

Bass Clef

Grand Staff

Music
α

中学年

リコーダーをまなぶ

演奏

皆さん、輪唱ってやったことがありますか。

二つに分かれて、少し遅れて歌いだす合唱ですね。

簡単な曲で練習しましょう。カエルの歌を、歌詞で歌ってみましょう。

先生
📢

かえるの歌

か　え　る　の　う　た　が　　き　こ　え　て　く　る　よ

ク　　ク　　ク　　ク　　　ケ　ロ　ケ　ロ　ケ　ロ　ク　ク　ク

次に、第1班と第2班が先に歌い、第2小節まで歌ったら、第3班と第4班が歌いだしてください。

はい、始めます。はい、できましたね。

では、これにリコーダーを付けますよ。

第1班はリコーダー、第2班は先の合唱、第3班は後のリコーダー、第4班は後の合唱です。

では始めてみましょう。

はい、繰り返しますよ。

Learning to play a Recorder 3

Let's Play

 Teacher

1 | Have you ever done a round chorus?

2 | It's a chorus in which you are divided into two groups and one group starts singing a little later.

3 | Let's practice with a simple song. Let's sing the frog song with the lyrics.

FROGGY'S SONG

Little   froggy's   little   song   Listen,   listen,   sing   along

Croak   Croak   Croak   Croak   Rabbit Rabbit Rabbit Rabbit Croak Croak Croak

4 | First, Group 1 and Group 2 will sing first, and after singing up to the second measure, Group 3 and Group 4 will start singing.

5 | Now, let's start. Okay, good job.

6 | Now, let's play the recorders with the song.

7 | Group 1 will play the recorder, Group 2 will sing the first chorus, Group 3 will play the second recorder, and Group 4 will sing the second chorus. Now let's begin.

8 | Okay, let's repeat.

中学年

歌唱

姿勢

先生

1 歌い方を学習しましょうね。

2 まず、姿勢が大切です。

3 立って歌う場合についてですが、全体の力を抜いて、背筋を伸ばして真っ直ぐに立って、体の力を抜きます。

4 両足を肩幅ぐらい開けて立ちます。

5 あごを引いて、目線は真っ直ぐよりやや上の方向を見ます。

6 姿勢が悪いと、いい声は出ませんよ。歌っていると、気づかないうちに、姿勢が悪くなってしまうことがあります。

7 猫背になっていたり、重心が後ろの方にいったり、膝が曲がっていないか気を付けてください。

8 では、座って歌う時の姿勢も学習しましょう。

9 全員、ソファミレド。

10 座るときは、椅子の前半分、背もたれにもたれかからないようにして、背筋は伸ばしてください。

11 座って歌うときも、立って歌うときも、まず息を十分に吸っておなかに空気をいっぱい入れて、「声を出そう」「歌おう」という気持ちで最初の声を出します。

Grade 3 & 4

Singing

Posture

Teacher

1. Let's learn how to sing.

2. First of all, posture is important.

3. When singing while standing, relax your entire body, stand up straight with your back straight and relaxed.

4. Stand with your feet shoulder-width apart.

5. Keep your chin down and your eyes looking slightly higher than straight ahead.

6. Bad posture will not produce a good voice. Singing can sometimes lead to bad posture without you even realizing it.

7. Be careful not to hunch over, or to keep your center of gravity backward, and make sure your knees are not bent.

8. Now let's also learn the posture for sitting and singing.

7. Everyone lets sing, So Fa Mi Re Do.

10. When you sit, do not lean against the front half or back of the chair, and instead keep your back straight.

11. When singing sitting or standing, first take a full breath and fill your stomach with air, and then make your first sound with the intention of "let's sing".

歌唱
歌い方

先生

1 次に、声の出し方です。

2 歌を歌うときって、自分の感情が入りますよね。

「メリーさんの羊」を暗い気持ちで歌おうなんて思いませんね。

3 気持ちよく、リズムに乗って楽しく歌いたいですね。

4 まず、皆さん、ニコッと笑ってみて。

5 そう、そのにこっとした笑顔で歌います。

6 ニコッと笑うと鼻の穴が開くでしょう。

7 そうすると沢山の息を吸ったり吐いたりできますから、声が出るようになります。

8 それと、目を大きく開けて、眉を上げてください。

9 大きな声を出せばいいというわけではありません。

10 お腹から、響くような声を出します。

11 そのためには口を大きく開けるんじゃなくて、のどの奥を広げます。

12 大きなあくびをしてみて。ほら！喉の奥が開いたでしょ。その感じです！

13 はい、その感じで、ヤッホーと声を出してみてください。はい！

このヤッホーとホーホーをオルガンの音に合わせて、高い音で出したり、長く出したり

14 しますよ。

15 はい、では、みんなドレミ！

16 言葉をもっとはっきりと発音して。オルガンの音に合わせてー。

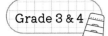

音楽

Grade 3 & 4

Singing

How to sing

Teacher

1 | Next, let's talk about the voice.

2 | When you sing a song, you have to put your feelings into it, don't you?

3 | You don't want to sing "Mary Had a Little Lamb" with a gloomy feeling, do you?

4 | First of all, everyone, try smiling.

5 | Yes, sing with that smiling face.

6 | Smile and your nostrils will open.

7 | This will allow you to inhale and exhale a lot, so you will be able to make a sound.

8 | Also, open your eyes wide and raise your eyebrows.

9 | It is not enough to make a loud sound.

10 | It is better that your voice resonate from the stomach.

11 | To do this, don't open your mouth wide, but expand the back of your throat.

12 | Try a big yawn. See? See how the back of your throat opens up. That's how it feels!

13 | Yes, try yoo-hoo like that. Go!

14 | Now let's make the yoo-hoo and hoo hoo sound with a higher pitch or longer in time with the organ.

15 | Yes, now, everyone Do Re Mi!

16 | Pronounce the words more clearly. Do it in time with the organ.

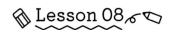

高学年

和音

基本

先生 📣

1 音楽はいろんな楽しみ方があります。

2 歌ったり、鳴らしたり、弾いたりです。

ピアノのような鍵盤楽器では、音を一度に重ねて引くことで響きを楽しむことができます。

3 いくつかオルガンで弾いてみましょうね。

4 これを和音といいます。

5 和音は高さの違う音を重ねますから、その高さによって、響き方はちがいます。

6 二つ以上の高さの音を重ねればなんでも和音になるというわけではありません。

3つの音で作る和音の場合、ドミソ、レファラ、ファラドなど、一個飛ばしに音を拾って

7 いきます。

8 この場合、和音の一番下の音を「根音」といいます。

9 根音はドレミファソラシありますから、3つの音の和音も7つできますね。

10 順番に1, 2, 3と並ぶのですが、数字はⅠ、Ⅱ、Ⅲと書きます。

11 このⅠ、Ⅱという書き方は初めて見ますね。

12 1, 2などの数を表すローマ数字です。1, 2, 3等の数字はアラビア数字ですね。

なぜ、ローマ数字で書いてあるかというと、ヨーロッパにアラビア数字が伝わる前から

13 今の音楽の元があって、ヨーロッパで使われていた数字がローマ数字だったからです。

14 ちなみに、ドレミファソラシはイタリア語です。

16 オルガンの一番左の音を聞いて下さい。ラの音ですね。

17 つまり、音のスタートは実はラからなんです。

18 ラシドレミファソが基本となって並んでいるんですね。

ですから、英語で表記するときも、日本に西欧音楽が伝えられたときも、初めの音のラに

19 最初の文字を当てはめる、つまり、ラにＡＢＣのＡ, イロハのイをあてて、

20 ラシドレミファソ＝ＡＢＣＤＥＦＧ＝イロハニホヘトと表記します。

日本では、ハ長調というドの音から始まる曲を基本として教えているので、

21 ドが最初の音だと思ってしまうと、音楽の勉強をするときに相当混乱します。

22 黒板に貼った表を見ながら説明します。

23 根音のポイントは、「ABC ･･･」が「ラ」から始まるってことです。

↖ 根音

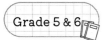

音楽

Music

Chords

Basic

1

Teacher

1 Music can be enjoyed in many ways.

2 It can be sung, made from different sounds, or played on an instrument.

3 On a keyboard instrument like the piano, you can enjoy the sound by playing overlapping sounds. Let's play some of these on an organ.

4 These are called chords.

5 Of course, now I am playing multiple sounds at the same time so they sound different.

6 It does not mean that combining two sounds makes it a chord.

7 In the case of a chord made of three notes, we pick up the notes one at a time, such as Do Mi So, Re Fa La, Fa La Do, and so on.

8 In this case, the lowest note of the chord is called the "root note".

9 For Do-Re-Mi-Fa-Sol-La-Si seven chords with three-root sounds can be made.

10 I will write these chords in the order 1, 2, and 3, but I will use the Roman numeral I, II, and III.

11 I guess you have never seen the numbers "I, II, and III", right?

They are Roman numerals used to write the numbers 1, 2, etc. In comparison,

12 the numbers 1, 2, 3, etc. are Arabic numerals.

The reason why they are written in Roman numerals is that today's music has existed even before Arabic numerals were introduced to Europe, and the numerals used in Europe were

13 Roman numerals.

14 By the way, Do Re Mi Fa Sol La Si is Italian.

15 Listen to the leftmost note on the organ. It is the "La" .

16 In other words, the organ starts with the la sound.

17 Wait — If we want to write So the basic line it is La Si Do Re Mi Fa.

So,when expressing music notes in English and when Western music was introduced to Japan,

19 "La" was written as A, which is the first letter in ABC and "I" which is the first syllabe in I Ro Ha.

20 In other words, La Si Do Re Mi Fa So＝ABCDEFG = I Ro Ha NI Ho He.

In Japan, songs are taught in the key of C major, which basically starts with the note Do,

21 so if you think Do is the first note, you will be quite confused when you study music.

22 I will explain this with a chart on the blackboard.

23 The main point is that the root "ABC..." starts with "La".

Root note

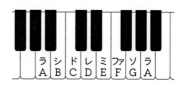

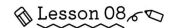

音楽

高学年

和音

和音別の音色

先生

1 この根音が「ド」であれば「C」。「レ」であれば「D」です。

2 ちなみに、「イロハ・・・」で言うこともあります（イ長調など）が、この場合も「ラ」から始まります。

3 また、根音をド＝C＝ハから始まる和音を順番にI度II度と呼んでいきます。

5 よく使われる和音は、1度（I C）、4度（IV F）、5度（V G）、5度の7（G7）の和音です。

6 C、F、G、G7はコードネームで伴奏の楽譜の小節の上などに付いています。

7 黒板の表を見てください。

8 オルガンで和音を順番に弾きますから、音をよく聞いてくださいね。

9 まずは、1度の和音です。1度は、ド・ミ・ソで、（和音の音）

10 1度の和音（I）は、根音を含んだ和音ですから、中心的な音、主音の性格を持ち、その調の中心となります。

11 安定した感じがします。

12 曲の始まりや終わりによく使われる和音です。

13 4度の和音（IV）です。どうですか。

14 1度に比べると、違和感がありますね。違和感があると、不安定な響きに聴こえますね。

15 次が、5度の和音（V）の和音です。

16 ドの音がないので、ますます違和感がありますね。不安定な響きです。

17 では、もっと不安な和音を弾いてみますよ。♪～。どうですか。

18 この和音は、5度の7の和音（V7）です。

19 さらに違和感を感じますね。

20 和音の中には、「B♭7」「D♯m」など、「♭」や「♯」がついて いることがあります。

21 この場合、「♭」や「♯」までが根音です。

22 なお、ラ♯とシ♭、レ♯とミ♭は同じ黒鍵盤ですよ。

23 こういう楽譜上では違う高さの音ですが、鍵盤図では同じ音を「異名同音」と言います。

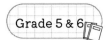

Grade 5 & 6

Chords

Sound

Teacher

Teacher: If the root note is a "Do," you would play a C note and

1 | if it is a "Re," you would play a D notes.

2 | By the way, the "I Ro Ha..." system (e.g., A major), also starts with "La".

3 | Chords that begin with the root note Do = C = / \are sometimes written as "I or II degree" chords.

5 | Commonly used chords are the first degree (I C), the fourth degree (IV F), and the fifth degree (VG).

| These are frequently witten as C, F, G, and G7 and you will see them attached to the bars of

6 | the accompaniment sheet music.

7 | Look at the chart on the blackboard.

8 | I'm going to play these on the organ, so please listen carefully.

I　II　III　IV　V　VI　VII　V$_7$

9 | First of all, the chord of the first degree, which is Do Mi and Sol(chord sound).

| The chord of the first degree (I) is a chord that contains a root note, so it has the character of

10 | a central note, the principal note, and is the main part of that chord .

11 | It has a stable feeling.

12 | It is a chord often used at the beginning or end of a piece.

13 | This is a chord of the fourth degree (IV). How does it sound?

| Compared to the first degree, it feels a bit strange. Because it is a bit strange, it sounds unstable,

14 | doesn't it?

15 | Next is the chord in the fifth degree (V).

16 | Since there is no Do note, it sounds even more odd . It sounds quite unstable.

17 | Now, let's play some more uneasy chords.   ♪ 〜What do you think?

V$_7$

18 | This is a 5th degree 7 chord (V7).

19 | It feels even more uncomfortable, doesn't it?

20 | Some chords have " ♭ " or " ♯ " attached to in them, such as "B ♭ 7" or "D ♯ m". In this case,

21 | the " ♭ " or "#" are also is the root note.

22 | In addition, "La ♯ " and "shi ♭ ", "re ♯ " and "Mi ♭ " are in the same black key on the keyboard.

| Although these might be written in different places on the score, they have the same pitch and

23 | are called enharmonic notes.

高学年

音程

基礎

先生 📢

1 では次に音程と学習します。音程は、二つの音の高さの違いです

ドとドは二つの音ですが、同じ高さなので、

2 音程が同じと言います。2つの音の隔たり。

3 つまり、音程とは、2つの音がどのくらい離れているかを、数字を使って示すことです。

たとえば、「ド」と「ソ」ならば、白い鍵盤は「ド・レ・ミ・ファ・ソ」を使うので、「5度」と

4 なります。

5 黒板の図を見てください。

6 鍵盤には、白鍵盤と黒鍵盤がありますね。

7 音程で度という場合、白い鍵盤で数えます。

「♯」や「♭」がついているときにも迷いますが、「○度」に関して言えば、「♯」や「♭」が

8 ついていないものとして数えます。

9 つまり、この二つの図は同じ5度です。

10 音程は、短とか長とか完全とか「短2度」や「完全5度」があります。

11 わかりやすいように、白鍵盤を○、黒鍵盤を●として、音程を書き出してみましょう。

「ドとレ」は、間に黒鍵があるので　○●○、「ミとファ」は、間に黒鍵がないので、○○と

12 なりますね。

両方とも2度なのですが、「ドとレ」は○●○、「ミとファ」は○○となり、●が多い分、

ドとレの間が長い2度ですね。これを長2度、白鍵盤だけで度を数える場合を短2度と

13 言います。

14 で、ここで応用。「ド♯とレ」は、短2度・長2度どちらでしょうか?

15 まず、調号(シャープ)を外して、「ドとレ」で考えると、「2度」ですね。

16 しかし階段で考えると、1段しか上がっていません。

17 つまり、「半音しか上がっていない」ということ。

これは、黒鍵を挟まない「短2度」(ミとファ)と同じ音の幅ですよね。

18 ということで、「短2度」となります。

19 和音を作るときに、短3度・長3度が必要になるので、しっかり理解しておきましょう。

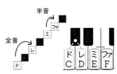 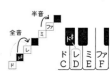

Grade 5 & 6

Intervals

Basic

Teacher

1　So let's move on to intervals. Interval is the difference in tone between two notes.

Do and Do are two notes, but they are the same tone,

2　so we say they have the same interval.

3　Interval is how far apart two notes are, amd to show that distance we use a number.

For example, if we consider "Do" and "So", they encompass 5 white keys between them

4　"Do Re Mi Fa So", so it is said to be a 5th interval.

5　Please look at the diagram on the blackboard.

6　There are white and black keys on the keyboard, right?

7　When we count "degree" in interval, we count the white keys.

Also, we don't count " ♯ " or " ♭ " when deciding the number of degrees. Instead, we ignore

8　the " ♯ " or " ♭ " and count from the preceding notes.

7　In other words, these two figures are the same 5 degrees.

An interval can be major, minor, or perfect, for example as a "minor 2nd degree"or

10　"perfect 5th degree".

To make it easier to understand, let's write out the intervals with the white keys as ◯ and

11　the black keys as ●.

The "Do and Re" are ◯●◯ because there is a black key in between, and the "Mi and Fa"

12　are ◯◯ because there is no black key in between.

Both are 2nd degrees, but the more "●" there are, the longer the interval between the notes

so Do and Re are called is called the major 2nd degree, and mi and fa are called the minor

13　2nd degree.

18　Now for a challenge. Which is "Do ♯ and Re", a minor second or major second?

First of all, if you remove the sharp sign (sharp) and think of it as the difference between

15　"Do and Re", it is "2 degrees".

16　However, if we think of it in terms of a staircase, it is only one step up.

17　In other words, "only a semitone higher.

This is the same sound width as the "minor 2nd degree" (mi and fa), which does not have

18　a black key in between. Therefore, it is a "minor 2nd degree".

When making chords, you will need the minor third degree and major third degree,

19　so make sure you understand them well.

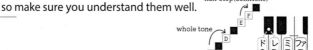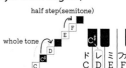

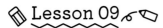

音楽

高学年

音程
和音の音色

先生

では、和音の音程を学習します。

「3度」は「ドミ」「レファ」「ミソ」「ファラ」「ソシ」「ラド」「シレ」など、和音でよく見かける組み合わせですね。

音の幅の決め手となるのは、間に黒鍵を挟まない「ミファ」「シド」を含むかどうかです。

別の言い方では、黒鍵を1つ挟むか、2つ挟むかです。

当然、黒鍵を2つ挟んだ方が「長く」なります。

黒板の図を見て下さい。

つまり基本は「黒鍵を1度しか挟まない」ものを「短3度」、「黒鍵を2度挟む」ものを「長3度」といいます。階段で言うと、短3度は、3段、長3度は4段上がることになりますね。

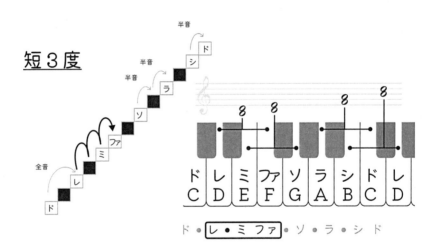

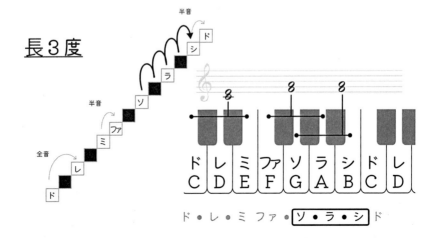

Grade 5 & 6

Intervals

Pitch of chords

Teacher

In this section, we will study the pitch of chords.

The "third degree" is a combination often seen in chords such as of "Do-Mi," "Re-Fa," "Mi-So," "Fa-la," "Sol-Si," "La-So," and "Si-Re,".

The decisive factor in determining the width of a note is whether or not it contains a black key in between the two notes such as "Mi-fa" or "Si-Do".

In other words, it is whether one or two black keys are sandwiched in between the notes.

Naturally, it is "longer" if two black keys are sandwiched.

Please see the diagram on the blackboard.

If we were to imagine it in terms of a staircase, the minor third degree is three steps up, and the major third degree is four steps up.

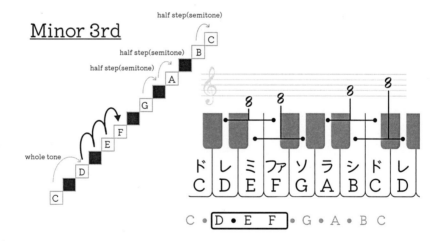

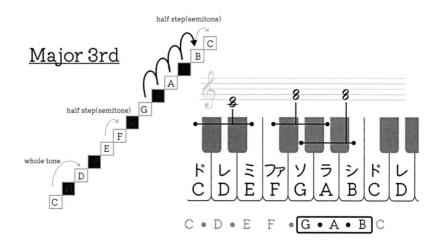

高学年

音程
和音の音色

先生

1　ところで、和音は３音以上で作りますね。

2　１度の和音は「ドミソ」ですね。

3　「ドとミ」、「ミとソ」の２音の音程は学習しましたね。

4　では、「ドミソ」の「ドとソ」の音程を考えましょう。

5　ドとソは、白鍵盤が５つですから、５度です。

6　一個ずつずらして、「レとラ」「ミとシ」「ファとド」「ソとレ」「ラとミ」「シとファ」も５度です。

7　この中で、仲間はずれがいるのですが、どれでしょうか？

8　「５度」の場合は、必ず「ミファ」「シド」のどちらかを挟みます。

9　そして、「シとファ」の組み合わせのときだけ、「シドレミファ」で、「ミファ」「シド」の両方を挟みますね。

10　つまり階段で言うと、「１段少なく」なっているのです。

11　そこで、「シとファ」を「減５度」、それ以外を「完全５度」と言います。

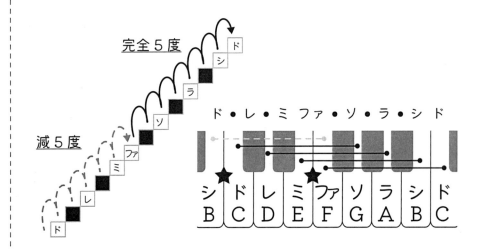

12　では、「ドとソ♭」「ドとソ♯」はどうでしょうか？

13　「ドとソ」は○●○●○○●○で完全５度ですね。

14　「ドとソ♭」は○が一つ減って○●○●○○●ですから、減５度、「ドとソ♯」は○●○●○○●○●で●が一つ増えますので、増５度となります。

Lesson 09

音楽

Grade 5 & 6

Intervals 2

Pitch of chords

Teacher

1. By the way, as you know chords are made of three or more notes.

2. The first is "Do-Mi-So".

3. You have learned the intervals of two notes, "Do and Mi" and "Mi and So".

4. Now, let's consider the intervals of "Do and So" in "Do Mi So.

5. Since there are five white keys for "Do" and "So", they are 5 degrees.

   Moving up the scale, the other fifth intervals would be one by one, "Re and La," "Mi and Si,"

6. "Fa and Do," "So and Re," "La and "Mi," and "Ci and Fa"

7. Which of these do not belong to the group?

8. The "fifth degree" always has either "Mi Fa" or "Si do." sandwiched inside.

   And only in the case of the combination of "Si and Fa," which is "Si Do Re Mi Fa," we have

9. sandwiched both "Mi Fa" and "Si do", right?

10. In other words, in terms of a staircase, there is "one less step".

    Therefore, "Si and Fa" are called a "diminished 5th degree" and the rest are called "perfect

11. 5th degree.

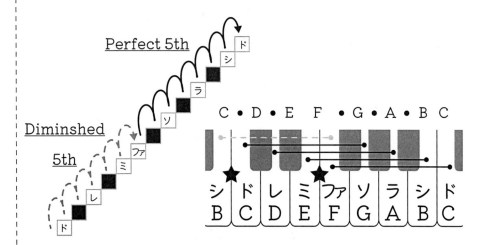

12. Then, how about "Do and Sol ♭ " and "Do and So ♯ "?

13. The "Do and So" is in the perfect fifth degree as shown ○●○●○○●○.

    The "Do and So ♭ " has one less ○ and is therefore a diminished 5th degree, ○●○●○○●,

    and the "Do and So ♯ " has one more ● and is therefore an augmented 5th degree,

16. as in ○●○●○○●○●.

高学年

柏と拍子

先生

1 一定の間隔で刻まれるリズムのその一つ一つを拍と言います。

2 周期的に強点（力点）をもってくり返される拍の集まりを拍子といいます。

3 1小節に拍が2つあれば2拍子、3つで3拍子、4つあると4拍子となります。

4 1つの小節に基本とする音符がいくつ分入っているかで拍子は決まります。

5 それぞれの曲の拍子は楽譜の最初に分数の形（拍子記号）で記してあります。

6 拍には強拍と弱拍があります。2拍子の行進曲では「イチ ニ イチ　ニ」と言ったり、3拍子のワルツの曲では「ズンチャッチャッ、ズンチャッチャッ」と言ったりします。

7 2拍子では「イチ」、3拍子では「ズン」の拍が強拍で、[ニ」や「チャッチャッ」は弱拍です。

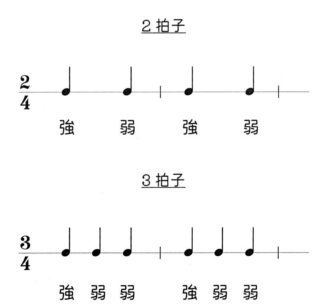

2 拍子

強　　弱　　強　　弱

3 拍子

強 弱 弱　　強 弱 弱

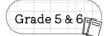

音楽

Music

Beats and time signatures

Grade 5 & 6

Teacher
📢

1. The regular division of a rhythm are called beats.

2. The pace at which these beats come is called the time signature.

3. If there are two beats in one bar, it is called a double, three is triple and four is quadruple.

4. The time signature is determined by the number of basic notes in the measure.

5. The time signature of each piece is indicated at the beginning of the score in the form of fractions (time signatures).

6. There are strong and weak beats: in a two-beat march, for example, we say "one two one two," the one is the strong or on-beat and the two is the weak or off beat.

7. And in a three-beat waltz tune we might say 'one two-three, one two-three', the first beat is the on-beat and the second and third are off-beats.

Two-Beat

$\frac{2}{4}$

Storng   Weak   Storng   Weak

Three-Beat

$\frac{3}{4}$

Storng Weak Weak   Storng Weak Weak

高学年

反復記号

先生

曲中で全く同じものを繰り返して演奏するとき、同じものを2回書くのは面倒なので省略して書く方法がいくつかあります。

それを反復記号と言うのですが、反復記号は音符に関するものと小節に関するものの2種類があります。

黒板の表を見て下さい。反復記号です。

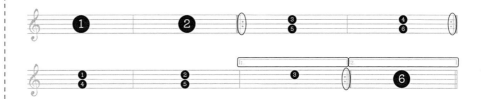

①から④まで演奏したらくり返しの記号がついているので、その記号ではさまれている部分をくり返します。

①から③まで演奏したらくり返しの記号がついています。このように1つだけついている場合は最初からくり返します。

そして2回目は「1（1番カッコ）はとばして「2（2番カッコ）を演奏して終わります。

最初から最後まで演奏します。

途中にFineという記号が出てきますが、気にしないで続けます。

最後にD.C（最初から）という記号が付いています。

従って初めに戻り演奏を続けます。

今度はFineまできたらここでおしまいという記号ですので終わります。

最初から最後まで演奏します。

途中に出てくる記号は気にせず続けます。

最後までくるとD.S.という記号が付いていますので、𝄋 まで戻り演奏を続けFineで終わります。

‖ ‖	リピート / Repeat
D.S.	ダル・セーニョ / Dal Segno（イタリア語）
D.C.	ダ・カーポ / Da capo（イタリア語）
𝄋	セーニョ / Segno（イタリア語）
Fine	フィーネ / Fine（イタリア語）

Lesson 11 音楽

Repetition marks

Teacher

When playing the exact same thing over and over in a piece, writing the same thing twice is bothersome, so it is written in abbreviated form.

There are several ways to do this. These are called repeat signs and there are two types, one for notes and the other for measures.

Look at the chart on the blackboard. These are the repetition marks.

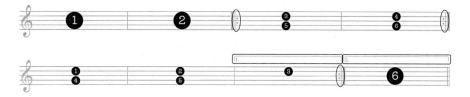

After playing ① through ④, you will see a repeat symbol, so repeat the part enclosed by the symbol.

If you play ① through ③, there is a repeat symbol. If there is only one symbol, repeat from the beginning.

When playing a second time, the "1" (the first bracket) is skipped and the "2" (the second bracket) is played to end the piece.

Let's play from the beginning to the end.

Then, you will see the word "Fine" in the middle, but don't worry about it.

The last note is marked D.C. (from the beginning).

Therefore, go back to the beginning and play again.

When you get to Fine, the symbol for "end here" appears, then you end the piece.

For the second one, we start by playing from the beginning to the end.

Do not worry about the symbols that appear in the middle of the piece this time, too.

When you reach the end, you will see the symbol D.S., so return to 𝄋 and continue playing, ending with Fine.

𝄇 𝄆	リピート / Repeat
D.S.	ダル・セーニョ / Dal Segno（イタリア語）
D.C.	ダ・カーポ / Da capo（イタリア語）
𝄋	セーニョ / Segno（イタリア語）
Fine	フィーネ / Fine（イタリア語）

高学年

日本の歌を楽しもう

先生

どの地方にも、昔から歌い継がれてきた音楽があります。

民謡とか子もり歌、わらべ歌と言われ、皆さんも小さいころから聴いたり歌ったりしてきた歌もあると思います。

全国でよく知られているものもあれば、その地方のみで歌われているものなど様々です。

民謡とは、日本各地で歌い継がれてきたもので、速さもゆっくりとしたものから速いものまで、また、さびしい曲調のもの、逆に陽気なもの、あるいは素朴な曲調のものまで様々です。

拍子も不規則なものが多いです。

みなさんが知っている民謡といえば、ソーラン節、刈干切り歌、黒田節などがあります。

子守歌には、その土地の人々の暮らしの中から生まれたものがたくさんあり、少しずつ形を変えながら今も歌い継がれています。

その数は 3,000 から 5,000 もあると言われています。

子どもを眠らせるための歌と労作歌としての子もり歌に分けられます。

子守歌はいつ頃からあったと思いますか。

日本で分かっているのは、古い文献には「聖徳太子の子守歌」とされる歌が記録されているそうです。

子守歌江戸時代末から急増しました。

商業や家内工業が活発化し、忙しい親が赤ちゃんの世話を家族以外の子もりに任せる風潮が高まりました。

子守りが労働となり、その子もりたちの間から多くの子もり歌が生まれました。

民謡や子守歌は、小節ごとの拍子が異なるものが多くあります。

ことに、拍子は、一つの曲の中で小節ごとに異なる曲が多くあります。

私たちが学習している音楽という科目は西欧音楽を基本としています。

日本人が西欧音楽を学ぶのは明治時代になってからですから、それ以前に日本で歌われてきたこれらの民謡や子守歌は、今の音楽のルールにはそぐわない部分もあります。

Grade 5 & 6

Let's enjoy Japanese songs

Teacher

In every region, there is music that has been sung from long ago.

They are called minyo (folk songs), komori (children's songs), and

warabeuta (folk songs for children), and I am sure that you have heard or sung some of them

since you were small children.

Some are well-known throughout Japan, while others are sung only in one region.

Minyo, or folk songs, have been sung throughout Japan and range in speed from slow to fast,

and in tune from dreary to cheerful or simple.

Many of them are also irregular in beat.

Some of the folk songs you may be familiar with include Soran-bushi, Karihagiri Uta,

and Kuroda-bushi.

There are many nursery songs that originated from the experiences of the local people,

and they are still sung today, changing their forms little by little.

It is said that there are between 3,000 and 5,000 of them.

They can be divided into two types of songs: songs for putting children to sleep and songs for labor.

When do you think lullbaies started?

What is known in Japan is that an old document records a song called

"Shotoku Taishi no Komori Uta," which is said to be a lullaby for Prince Shotoku.

The number of nursery songs increased rapidly from the end of the Edo period (1603-1867).

With the rapid development of the Commerce and cottage industry there was a growing trend

for busy parents to entrust the care of their babies to babysitters outside the family.

This child-care became a form of labor, and many songs about child-care emerged from these

mothers.

Many folk songs and lullabies have different time signatures.

In particular, there are many songs that have different time signatures within a single song.

In this class, we are mainly studying western music.

Since Japanese people did not learn Western music until the Meiji era (1868-1912),

these folk songs and lullabies that were sung in Japan before that time do not fit the rules of

today's music in some respects.

家 庭 科

subject 8

Home Economics

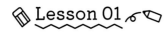 **Lesson 01**

調理実習

高学年

準備

先生

1　小学生になって、給食当番をしたり、教室の掃除をしたりしてきましたが、上級生になりましたから、調理や縫物といった日常の暮らしに役立つ学習を加えていきます。

2　まずは、調理を学習しましょう。

3　エプロンとマスク、三角巾は持ってきましたね。

4　それと爪は切ってきましたか。

5　爪がのびていないか確認して、伸びている人は爪切りを貸しますから切ってください。

6　まずは調理するための道具の説明と調理の準備をします。

7　机の上に、まな板と包丁を並べてください。

8　また板とはそのうえで、野菜を切ったり、魚をさばいたりしますから、衛生的でなくてはいけません。

9　取り扱いを説明します。

10　まず、水で表面を濡らします。その後固く絞ったふきんで拭いてください。

11　調理が終わったら、洗剤をつけたスポンジたわしで擦ります。

12　水ですすぎ、その後、熱湯を全体にかけてください。熱湯をかけるのは、ウイルスは熱に弱いからです。

13　終わったら、窓側の棚において乾燥させます。

14　日が当たり、風通しがよいので、殺菌になります。

15　次に包丁です。

16　包丁については、刃先を人に向けないこと、他の人に渡すときは手渡しでなく、台の上に置いて渡すこと、持ったまま動きまわらないこと、落ちやすいところに置かないことを守ってください。

17　包丁を洗うときは、流しに置いて、たわしで洗います。

18　包丁の持ち方ですが、利き手の人差し指と親指で柄を包むように持ちます。

19　もう片方の手は材料を支えますが、指は猫の手です。

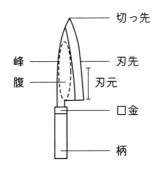

切っ先
峰　　　　　　刃先
腹　　　　　　刃元
　　　　　　　口金
柄

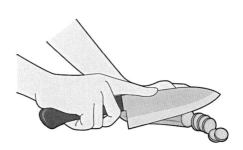

 Grade 5 & 6

Cooking Lessons

Preparation for Cooking Practice

Teacher

As elementary school students, you have been doing lunch duty and cleaning classrooms. However now that you are in the upper grades, we will add useful everyday life skills such as

1 cooking and sewing.

2 First, Let's learn how to cook.

3 You have brought an apron, a mask, and a bandana.

4 Have you cut your nails?

5 If not, we will lend you a nail clipper.

6 First, we will explain the tools for cooking and prepare the ingredients.

7 First place the cutting board and knives on the table.

8 The board is also used for cutting vegetables and cleaning fish, so it must be sanitary.

9 Here are some instructions on how to handle it.

10 First, rinse the cutting board with water. Then wipe with a tightly wrung dishcloth.

11 After cooking, you will wash it with a sponge and soap.

12 Rinse with cold water and then pour boiling water over the entire area. The reason for pouring boiling water is that viruses are sensitive to heat.

13 When you are finished, place them on a window shelf to dry.

14 The sunlight and good ventilation will help to kill any viruses.

15 Next is the knife.

16 When you hand a knife to another person, do not pass it to him or her by hand, but place it on a table for them to pick up. Do not move around with a knife in your hand, and do not leave it where it can easily fall off a surface.

17 When washing knives, place them in the sink and wash them with a scrubbing brush.

18 On how to hold a knife: hold the knife so that the index finger and thumb of the dominant hand encircle the handle.

19 The other hand supports the ingredient, with curled fingers like a cat's claw.

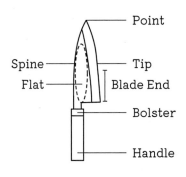

Point

Spine — Tip
Flat — Blade End

Bolster

Handle

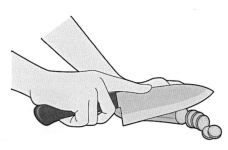

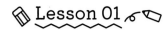
 高学年

調理実習

ご飯を炊く

先生

まず、お米ですが、計量カップで山盛りにお米を取り、へらなどで平らにします。
これで、お米200mlです。

お米をボールに入れて、洗います。洗ったら、ざるに入れて水を切り、
その後このガラス鍋に入れます。

そこまでおわったら、30分そのまま待ちます。

それでは、待っている間に味噌汁を作りましょう。今日のみそ汁の実はとあぶらあげと
長ネギです。

まず、だしを取ります。煮干しの頭とはらわたをとり、手で3つか4つにちぎってください。

なべに、班の人数に1人分170mlで計算した水を入れ、煮干しを入れます。

そしたら、強火にかけて、沸騰したら中火にして5分待ちます。

待っている間に、具を切ります。具の切り方ですが、油揚げは短冊切り、長ネギは小口切り
をします。見てください、どちらの時も、支える方の手の指は猫の手ですよ。

そろそろ5分経ちましたね、そしたら、火を止めて、穴あきお玉で、煮干しを取り出します。
だし汁を1カップ分汲んでボールに入れ、そのなかに、
人数分に一人大さじ5分の4杯（15g）のみそを入れて溶きます。

鍋のなかに実をいれて煮ますが、火は弱火です。

ねぎはすぐに煮えます。

みそを入れて煮れば、みそ汁は出来上がりです。

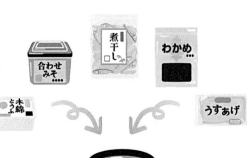

Grade 5 & 6

Cooking Lessons 2

Cooking Rice

Teacher

1. First, take a heaping pile of rice in a measuring cup and flatten it with a spatula. This is 200 ml of rice.

2. Put the rice in a bowl and wash it. After washing, put it in a colander to drain the water, then put it in this glass pot.

3. Once that is done, wait for 30 minutes.

4. Now let's make miso soup while we wait. Today's miso soup is deep-fried tofu and green onion.

5. First, take the dashi. Remove the heads and guts of the dried sardines and tear them into three or four pieces by hand.

6. Fill a pot with water calculated at 170 ml per person for the number of people in the group, and add the dried sardines.

7. Then, put it over high heat, and when it comes to a boil, reduce the heat to medium and wait for 5 minutes.

8. While waiting, cut the ingredients. As to how to cut them, cut the deep-fried tofu into strips and the green onion into small pieces. Look, in both cases, the fingers of the supporting hand are in the shape of a cat's paw.

9. After 5 minutes have passed, turn off the heat and remove the dried fish with a ladle with holes. Dissolve 1 cup of dashi broth in a bowl, adding 4/5 tablespoons (15 g) of miso for each person in the bowl.

10. Place the ingredients in a pot and bring to a simmer, but over low heat.

11. Green onion cooks quickly.

12. Add miso and simmer, and miso soup is ready.

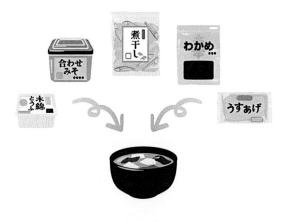

高学年

調理実習
みそ汁を作る

先生

1　だしをいれたみそ汁と出しをいれていないみそ汁をみんなで飲み比べてみましょうね。

2　どうですか。

　出し入りがおいしいでしょ。日本食という食事は、昔、主食のお米と野菜でした。

3　どのようにしてこの野菜をおいしく食べるかという工夫がなされました。

　煮干しや鰹節、コンプ、しいたけ等は煮ると、その中にあるうまみ成分が取り出せます。

4　日本食は、そのうまみ成分を料理の味の基礎とする食文化です。

5　そろそろ、30分経ちましたね。

6　では、コンロに火をつけてください。沸騰するまで強火でいいですよ。

7　湯気じゃなくて、水蒸気ですね。水蒸気が出てきたら火を弱くしてください。

8　中火で15分炊きます。

9　15分経ちましたから、10分間水気がなるなるまで弱火にしてください。

10　その間に、先ほどの手順で味噌汁を作ります。出しを取って、実を切ってください。

11　10分経ちましたら、火を止めて、10分間蒸らします。

12　その間に、みそを溶かして、実を入れた鍋にみそを入れて味噌汁を作ってください。

13　味噌汁の火を止めて、茶碗と汁椀を準備してください。

14　ご飯をしゃもじで取り分けて、お玉で味噌汁をよそってください。

15　食べ終わったら、片づけますよ。まな板の片付け方は分かっていますね。

　包丁は、まな板の上で、水道水で片面ずつ洗剤をつけたスポンジたわしで洗った後、

16　ふきんで水分を取ります。

17　流しやコンロは、雑巾できれいに拭いてください。

18　ガスコンロの元栓を閉めて、ごみは分別して捨ててください。

　手を石鹸でよく洗い、キッチンタオルで拭いてから、エプロン、三角巾を取って、

19　たたんでください。

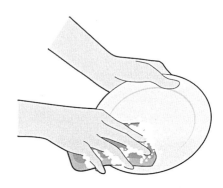

Cooking Lessons

Miso Soup

Teacher

1. Let's compare a sip of miso soup with dashi and without dashi.

2. How do you like it?

3. With dashi it's delicious, isn't it? In the past, Japanese food consisted of rice and vegetables as the staple food. So, we tried to think of ways to make these vegetables taste better.

When dried sardines, dried bonito flakes, kelp, shiitake mushrooms, etc. are boiled, it brings out a savory flavor. In Japanese food culture the umami component is the basis of the flavor

4. of the dish.

5. It's been almost 30 minutes.

6. Now, light the stove. You can use high heat until it boils.

7. It's not steam, it's vapor. When vapor appears, turn down the heat.

8. Cook over medium heat for 15 minutes.

9. After 15 minutes, reduce the heat to low for 10 minutes until it becomes steamy.

Meanwhile, make miso soup according to the previous procedure. Take out the soup stock and

10. cut the ingredients.

11. After 10 minutes, turn off the heat and let it steam for 10 minutes.

12. In the meantime, dissolve the miso and add it to the pot with the ingredients to make miso soup.

13. Turn off the heat of the miso soup and prepare the rice bowls and soup bowls.

14. Use a rice scoop to serve the rice and a ladle to serve the miso soup.

When you're done eating, Let's put everything away. You know how to put away the cutting

15. board.

Wash both sides of the knives on a cutting board with a wet sponge that has detergent on it,

16. then pat dry with a dish towel.

17. Sinks and stoves should be wiped clean with a rag.

18. Please turn off the main valve of the gas stove, separate the garbage and dispose of them.

Wash your hands well with soap and dry them with a kitchen towel, then take your apron and

19. bandana and fold them.

調理実習

ゆでる

先生

1 今日はゆでるという調理をやってみましょう。

2 まずは、皆さんもよく食べるゆで卵を作ってみましょう。

3 まず、卵を洗います。卵の殻を食べるわけではありませんが、できるだけ料理の材料に付着している病原菌を洗い落としておくためです。

4 次に、鍋に水を差しますが、水の量は卵をいれて、卵がかぶるくらいです。

5 あまり多くしないでください。時間もかかりますし、沸騰しますから、水の量が多いと、鍋から吹き出して、火が消えたり、はねてきた熱湯でやけどをしたりすることもあります。

6 今から、火をつけて茹でますが、ゆでる時間によって、ゆで卵はとろとろの半熟から固いものまでできます。

7 今日はかたゆでたまごを作ります。

8 ゆでる時間は、水が沸騰してから10分間です。

9 時間を測る人を各班で決めてください。では、火をつけますよ。

10 10分経ったら、火を止めて、卵を取り出しますが、熱湯になっていますから、絶対に指を入れたりしてはダメですよ。穴あきお玉で取り出します。

11 そしたら、水の入ったボールにいれて卵を冷ましから殻をとります。

12 出来ましたね。では、青菜をゆでてみましょう。

13 分量は、一人2株です。自分の分を水で洗ってください。

14 野菜ですから土がついていることもありますからよく洗ってください。

15 ゆで卵は最初から水に入れて沸騰させましたが、青菜やホウレン草のような葉っぱを食べる野菜の場合は、湯を沸かして沸騰してからいれて、短時間でゆでます。

16 野菜をいれると温度が下がりますから、鍋の水は多めに入れてください。

17 お湯が沸騰してきましたか。そしたら、塩をひとつかみ入れてください。

18 混ぜる必要ありませんよ。次に青菜を茎の方から入れてください。

19 30秒くらいで、箸で引き上げて、ボールに水に浸けてください。

20 水に浸けると、青菜の緑色があざやかになるだけでなく、しぶ味やえぐみなどのアクを取り除けます。

21 ボールから取りだして、揃えて軽く絞って水気をとってから、まな板に載せてください。

22 4～5cmに切りそろえて、皿に盛りつけてください。

23 もりつけたら、上に鰹節を少しかけて、醤油をすこし垂らして味付けをしてください。

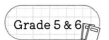
Grade 5 & 6

Cooking Lessons

Boil

Teacher

1 | Today let's try cooking by boiling.

2 | First, let's make boiled eggs, which you often eat.

First, wash the eggs. Although we do not eat the eggshells, we do so in order to wash off
3 | as much of the pathogens as possible from the cooking ingredients.

4 | Next, fill the pan with water, but only enough to cover the eggs. Do not use too much.

It takes a long time to boil, and if the amount of water is too much, the water in the pot may
5 | extinguish the fire, or you may be scalded by the boiling water that splashes out.

Now we are going to turn on the fire and boil the eggs. Depending on the boiling time,
6 | boiled eggs can range from soft-boiled to hard-boiled.

7 | Today we will make hard-boiled eggs.

8 | Boil the eggs for 10 minutes after the water comes to a boil.

9 | Each group will decide who will measure the time. Now, let's start the fire.

After 10 minutes, turn off the heat and remove the eggs, but never put your fingers in the water
10 | because it is now boiling hot. Take them out with a ladle with holes.

11 | Then, place the eggs in a bowl of water to cool before removing the shells.

12 | You've done it. Now let's boil some greens.

13 | The quantity is 2 plant bunches per person. Wash your portion with water.

14 | Since they are vegetables, they may have soil on them, so please wash them well.

For boiled eggs, put them in water and then start boiling. For leafy vegetables such as greens
and spinach, bring the water to a boil and then add them to the water and boil them in for
15 | a short time.

16 | The temperature drops as the vegetables are added, so more water should be added to the pot.

17 | Has the water come to a boil? Then add a pinch of salt.

18 | You don't need to mix. Next, add the greens, stem side up.

19 | After about 30 seconds, pull them up with chopsticks and soak them in a bowl of water.

Soaking in water not only brightens the green color of the greens, but also removes
20 | the bitterness and harsh taste from the greens.

21 | Remove from the bowl, place on a cutting board, and cut into 4-5 cm pieces and place on a plate.

When the fish is ready to be served, sprinkle a little dried bonito flakes on top and season with
22 | a dash of soy sauce.

家庭科

Home Economics

高学年

裁縫

手縫い

先生

1. 人間は進化の過程で早い段階で、体を毛に覆われる進化を捨てました。

2. その結果、寒さを防ぐために何かを纏うことが必要になりました。

3. 遥か昔は動物の皮を身にまとっていましたが文明の進歩とともに繊維を織った布を身にまとい、さらに持ち運ぶための袋を作るようになりました。

4. 布を織る、さらに織った布を裁断して着やすい服にするためには、糸で縫い合わせるという技術が必要です。

5. 縫い方の基本を学習していきましょう。

6. まず、裁縫セットの中から、縫い針を1本、針刺し、糸切りばさみ、手縫い糸、指ぬきを出してください。

7. 縫い針は糸を通す穴があるものですね。

8. 針は、落とすとわからなくなりますから、裁縫セットからだしたらすぐに針刺しにさしてください。

9. 利き手の中指に指ぬきをつけてください。指ぬきは針が指や手に当たるところを保護します。

10. では、手縫い糸薪から、糸を伸ばしてください。

11. そして糸の先端を糸切りばさみで斜めになるように切ります。

12. 切った先端を、針の穴に通します。

13. 針の真ん中あたりを左手の親指と人差し指でつまんで、動かないようにして、糸を穴に通します。

14. 通したら、糸が穴から落ちないように10cm くらい出しておいて、手縫い糸巻きから30cm 位のところで切ってください。

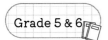

Sewing

Basics

Teacher

In social studies, you have learned about life in the past, right? Early in our evolutionary process, humans gradually lost the covering of hair over their bodies.

As a result, it became necessary to clothe ourselves with something to protect us from the cold. In the far distant past, we used to wear animal skins, but as civilization progressed, we began to wear cloth woven from fibers and even made bags to carry them in.

Weaving cloth and cutting the woven cloth into wearable clothing requires the skill of sewing with thread.

Let's learn the basics of sewing.

First, please take out one sewing needle, a needle holder, thread trimming scissors, hand sewing thread, and a thimble from your sewing kit set.

The sewing needle should have a hole for the thread.

The needle will be lost if you drop it, so put it in the needle holder as soon as you take it out of the sewing kit.

Wear a thimble on the middle finger of your dominant hand. The thimble protects the needle from pricking your finger or hand.

Now, from the hand sewing thread spool, stretch the thread.

Then cut the end of the thread at an angle with thread scissors.

Thread the cut end through the hole in the needle.

Pinch the middle of the needle with the thumb and forefinger of your left hand to keep it from moving, and thread the thread through the hole.

After threading, pull the thread out about 10 cm so that it does not fall out of the hole, and cut it off about 30 cm from the hand sewing thread roll.

高学年

裁縫
運針

先生

1. 糸を針に通したら、長い方の糸の端を結んで、塗った糸が抜けださないようにします。

2. これを玉結びといいます。いいですか、

3. 糸の端を人差し指の先に1回巻きつけます。

4. そして、親指で糸を押えます。

5. 人さし指をずらすようにして、輪になった糸を数回より合わせます。

6. より合わさった所を中指で押さえ、そのまま糸を引くと玉結びの出来上がりです。

7. しっかり糸を引いて、かたく結んでくださいね。

8. では、実際に布を使って、針で縫ってみましょう。

9. 針を持たない方の手は親指と人差し指で布をつかみ、針をもっている方の手は、人差し指と中指で布をつかみます。

10. 右手と左手の間隔は10cm位です。

11. 針を布の上から斜め前に差し、布より針の3分の1くらいが出たら、布を動かして、針の先を布に通して上に針が出るようにします。

12. そしてもう一度布を通して下に針をだし、今度は針を持つ手を布から離して、布の下から針を掴み、糸が玉結びで止まるまで引っ張ります。

13. その要領で、布の端まで縫ってきたら、布の上で針を出して、糸を通して折れ曲がったところを両手で伸ばしたら糸を玉止めします。

14. 玉止めの方法ですが、糸の出ている根元に針をあて、親指と人さし指で押えます。

15. 針先に2回くらい糸を巻き、親指で押えて、針を引き抜きます。

16. 糸端を少し残して、はさみで切ると完成です。

1
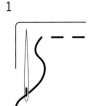

2

3
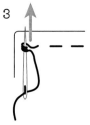

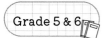
Grade 5 & 6

Sewing

Hand Movement

Teacher

1. After threading the needle, tie off the longer end of the thread to prevent the thread from
2. falling out. This is called a thread knot. Ready?
3. Wrap the end of the thread around the tip of your index finger once.
4. Then, hold the thread with your thumb.
5. Roll your index finger over the thread several times to twist it together.
6. Hold the twisted thread with your middle finger and pull the thread to complete the knot.
7. The knot is done. Pull the thread tight so as to tie the knot firmly.
8. Now, let's try sewing with a needle using an actual cloth.

The hand that does not hold the needle should grip the cloth with the thumb and forefinger,
9. and the hand that holds the needle should hold the cloth with the thumb and forefinger.

10. The distance between the right hand and the left hand should be about 10 cm.

Insert the needle diagonally forward over the cloth, and when about one-third of the needle

emerges from the cloth, move the cloth so that the tip of the needle comes up through
11. the cloth.

Then, again insert the needle through the cloth and bring it out at the bottom. This time,

remove the hand holding the needle from the cloth, grasp the needle from under the cloth,
12. and pull the thread until it stops at the thread knot.

When you have sewn to the edge of the cloth in this manner, bring the needle out above

the cloth, pass the thread through and stretch the folded part with both hands, and then stop
13. the thread with a thread knot.
14. Place the needle at the base of the thread and press down with your thumb and index finger.

Wrap the thread around the tip of the needle twice, press down with your thumb, and pull
15. the needle out.
16. Cut the end of the thread with scissors, and you are done.

1

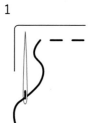

2

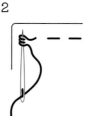

3

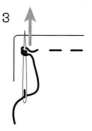

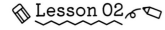

高学年

裁縫
縫い方

先生

裁縫の歴史は1000年以上前にさかのぼります。縫い合わせる素材の質や厚み、目的等よって縫い方にも工夫がされています。

今日は代表的な縫い方を学習しましょう。

まず、本返し縫いをやってみましょう。

丈夫に縫いたいときに使います。

1針ごとに布を左右に引いて布のしわを取るのがコツです。

布の下から針を刺し、上から1針分戻って針を刺し、下から2針分進んで針を出します。

これを連続して繰り返し、縫い終わりは布の裏で玉どめをします。

針ゆび抜きで針のお尻を押さないと、手をケガしますよ。

玉止めするときは、糸を針にゆるく巻き付けては止めが作れません。

巻いたところを親指で押さえて、ちょっとそれだとできないですね。

巻く場所が針の先の方過ぎます。

もっと真ん中あたりで巻かないと、親指で押さえたときに針の先が隠れて、針が抜けないでしょ。

次は、半返し縫いです。

針目をそろえるために、網目を利用します。1針ごとに布を左右に引いて布のしわを取るのがコツです。

布の下から針を刺し、上から1針の半分戻って針を刺し、下から1針分進んで針を出します。

これを繰り返し、縫い終わりは布の裏で玉どめをします

今日の学習の最後は、かがり縫いです。

ほつれやすい布端を始末する時に使います。針目をそろえるには、針の進み方、布端から針を刺す寸法をそろえることがポイントです。

二枚の布を重ね、布の間から針を出します。(玉結びを隠します)

二枚の布端を巻くようにかがります。縫い終わりは布の間で玉どめをします。

半返し縫い

かがり縫い

Sewing

How to sew

Teacher

The history of sewing dates back more than a thousand years. Depending on the quality and thickness of the materials being sewn together, as well as the purpose of the sewing, there have been many different ways to sew.

Today, we will learn some typical sewing methods.

First, let's try the main backstitch.

You should use it when you want to sew sturdily.

The trick is to take out the wrinkles of the fabric by pulling the fabric left and right after each stich.

Stick the needle from the bottom of the cloth, go back one stitch from the top, and go forward two stitches from the bottom. Take out the needle.

Repeat this process continuously, and at the end of the stitching, make a thread knot at the back of the cloth.

If you don't push the butt of the needle with the thimble, you will injure your hand.

When you make a thread knot, you cannot make the knot by wrapping the thread loosely around the needle.

You have to hold the point where the thread is wrapped around the needle with your thumb, but that's not enough. Don't wind it too far toward the end of the needle.

If you don't wind it more in the middle, the tip of the needle will be hidden when you hold it down with your thumb, and you won't be able to pull the needle out.

The next step is to do a half back stitch.

Use the mesh to align the stitches; the trick is to pull the fabric from side to side after each stitch to remove wrinkles from the fabric.

Stick the needle in from the bottom of the cloth, come back half a stitch and then stick it in again.

One half stitch back from the top, and one stitch forward from the bottom.

Repeat this process, and at the end of the stitch, make a thread knot at the back of the cloth.

The last part of today's study is the kagarinui(over hand stitch).

This is used to finish the frayed edges of fabric. In order to align the stitches, it is important to align the way the needle advances and the distance of the needle from the edge of the cloth.

Lay the two pieces of cloth on top of each other, and bring the needle out from between the cloths.   (This hides the thread knot.)

Wind the two fabric edges together. When you finish sewing, make a thread knot between the fabrics.

Short rows (in sewing)

Kagarinui(over casting stitch)

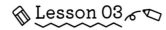
高学年

ミシン

操作方法

先生

1. 今日は、この電動ミシンの使い方を学習します。

2. では、ミシンに糸を掛けていきましょう。

3. ミシンで縫うために、二本の糸をかけます。電源は入れません。

4. 糸をかけるときに、電源が入っていると指を縫ってしまうなど思わぬ事故につながりやすいので、糸をかけるときは電源を切ってください。

5. 針穴に糸を通すときは、電源が入っていないと、ミシンの電気がつかず、針穴が見えにくくなります。

6. まず、下糸ですが、ボビンに巻き、ボビンをボビンケースに入れます。

7. 糸の端を糸調子ばねの下に通します。

8. ボビンケースをかまにカチッと音がするまで入れます。

9. 上糸ですが、電源が入っていないことを確認して、「押さえ上げ」を上げ、糸こまを「糸立て棒」にセットします。

10. 糸を「糸案内版」に右の図のようにかけ、糸を「糸案内板」に沿って下まで下ろし、左上に引き上げます。

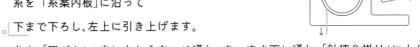

11. 糸を「天びん」の穴に右から左へと通し、まっすぐ下に通し、「針棒糸掛け」に上から通し、前から後ろに向かって針に糸を通します。

12. では、もう一度説明しますね。説明に合わせてやってみてください。

13. よいですか。では、下糸を出します。出し方は、上糸をもって、はずみ車を手前に回すと、下糸が上糸にからまって上がってきます。そしたら、上糸を引き上げて下糸とそろえて10cm位で切り、おさえの下を通して向こう側へ回します。

Sewing Machine

How to sew

Teacher

1. Today you will learn how to use this electric sewing machine.

2. Now, let's thread the sewing machine.

3. Apply two threads to sew on the sewing machine. Do not turn on the power.

4. During threading, if the power is on, it can easily lead to unexpected accidents such as sewing a finger. Therefore, please turn off the power when you thread.

5. When threading the needle hole, if the power is not on, the light will not turn on and the needle hole will be difficult to see.

6. First, the lower thread is wound onto a bobbin and the bobbin is placed in the bobbin case.

7. Pass the end of the thread under the thread adjustment spring.

8. Insert the bobbin case into the bobbin until it clicks into place.

9. As for the upper thread, make sure that the power is not on, raise the "lift lever" and set the thread piece on the "thread stand bar."

10. Hang the thread over the "thread guide plate" as shown in the figure on the right,lower the thread down along the "thread guide plate" and pull it up to the upper left.

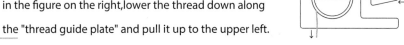

11. Thread the yarn through the hole in the "balance" from right to left, straight down, through the "needle bar threader" from the top, and thread the needle from front to back.

12. Now, let me explain again. Please try to follow the explanation.

13. Now, let's take out the lower thread. To take out the upper thread, hold the upper thread and turn the wheel toward you, and the lower thread will be caught in the upper thread and come up. Then, pull up the upper thread, align it with the lower thread, cut it off at about 10 cm, and pass it under the sheathing and turn it to the other side.

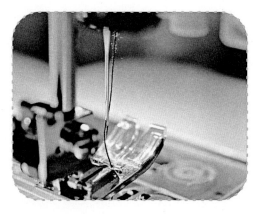

高学年

ミシン

縫製

先生

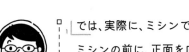

1 では、実際に、ミシンで縫ってみましょう

　ミシンの前に、正面を向いてきちんと座ってください。電動ミシンはスイッチがきれないと
2 針が動き続けます。

3 よそみをしないで、布と針から離さないようにしてください。

4 大けがをしてしまいます。

　まず、ミシンの押えを上げて、布のぬい始めに針をさし、お さえをゆっくりおろして布に
5 手を添えて下さい。

6 はい、縫い始めます。針が印の上を通るように、しっかり見 てぬってください。

　印が見えにくい時は、おさえの端を布の目印に平行に沿わせてぬうと、まっすぐ
7 ぬえますよ！

8 はずみ車を手前に回し、てんびんを一番上に上げしっかり見 てぬってください。

9 おさえをあげて、布を向こう側へ引っぱり出し上糸と下糸を 10cm 位引き出して切ります。

10 では、直線の縫い方がわかりましたから、方向転換して別の面の縫い方を学習しましょう。

11 角で方向転換しますよ。まず、布に針を刺したまま、押えをあげて、布の向けを変えます。

　左手をわざわざミシンの外側から回さなくても、ミシンの間から手を入れて、向けを
12 変えていいですよ。

13 はい、向きが変わったら、おさえをゆっくり下して、縫い始めてください。

14 はい、端まで行きましたね。ここで、糸を切ってしまうと、糸がほつれてしまいますね。

15 手縫いのとこは玉どめ留で、留めますね。

16 ミシンの場合は、返し縫いと言って、縫い目を戻して縫います。

17 送り調整ダイヤルを押しながら縫ってください。

Sewing Machine

Sewing

Teacher

1. let's sew on your sewing machine.

2. Please sit properly in front of the sewing machine, facing forward. The electric sewing machine continues to move the needle unless the switch is turned off.

3. Do not lean over and do not let go of the fabric or the needle.

4. You could be seriously injured.

5. First, raise the presser of the sewing machine, insert the needle at the point where you will begin stitching the cloth, and then slowly lower the rest and place your hand on the cloth.

6. All right, start sewing. Watch carefully so that the needle passes over the mark.

7. If it is difficult to see the mark, you can sew in a straight line by drawing the edge of the sheath parallel to the mark on the fabric!

8. Turn the wheel toward you, raise the thread take up lever to the top and look at it carefully.

9. Raise the restraints and pull the cloth to the other side, and then pull the upper and lower threads about 10cm apart. Pull out and cut.

10. Now that we know how to sew in a straight line, let's change direction and learn how to sew in the other direction.

11. We will change direction at the corner. First, with the needle still in the fabric, raise the presser to change the direction of the fabric.

12. You don't have to turn your left hand from the outside of the machine, but you can change the direction by inserting your hand between the machines.

13. Once the orientation is changed, slowly lower the clamps and begin sewing.

14. You have reached the end. If you cut the thread at this point, the thread will fray.

15. If you are sewing by hand, you need to fasten the thread with a thread knot.

16. On a sewing machine, the seam is called a backstitch.

17. Let's go back to sewing. Sew while pressing the feed adjustment dial.

家庭科の単語集

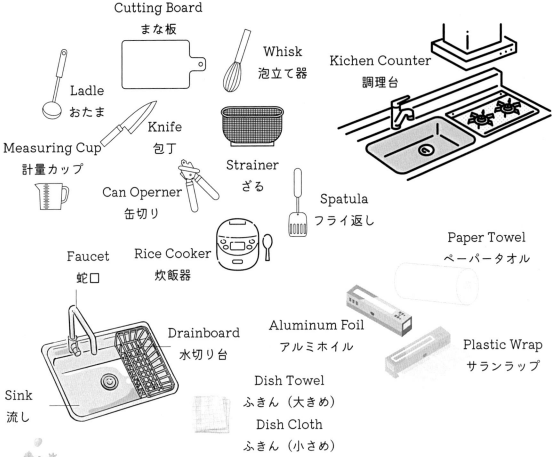

Cutting Board
まな板

Whisk
泡立て器

Kichen Counter
調理台

Ladle
おたま

Knife
包丁

Measuring Cup
計量カップ

Can Operner
缶切り

Strainer
ざる

Spatula
フライ返し

Paper Towel
ペーパータオル

Faucet
蛇口

Rice Cooker
炊飯器

Aluminum Foil
アルミホイル

Plastic Wrap
サランラップ

Drainboard
水切り台

Dish Towel
ふきん（大きめ）

Dish Cloth
ふきん（小さめ）

Sink
流し

Grill
(直火で)焼く

Toast
(オーブンで)焼く

Roast
(オーブンで)焼く

Bake
(パン/ケーキを)焼く

Low Heat
弱火

Midium Heat
中火

High Heat
強火

Boil / 茹でる

Blanch / 湯どうしする

Steam / 蒸す

Fly / 油で揚げる

Strain / 裏ごしする

Heat up / レンジでチンする

Grate / すりおろす

Sprinkle salt / 塩をふる

Skim / アクをとる

教職英語検定受検ガイド

教職英語検定実施要領

📖 LEVEL 🏷

基礎 ─┬─ リスニング
　　　└─ 筆記

標準 ─┬─ リスニング
　　　├─ 筆記
　　　└─ 英作文

実践 ─┬─ ^{一次} リスニング
　　　├─ 筆記
　　　├─ 英作文
　　　└─ ^{二次} グループ討議

📖 検定日程 🏷

年2回実施

第1回 ┤ 一次　1月第4日曜日
　　　└ 二次　2月第4日曜日
　　　　　　　※実践レベルのみ

第2回 ┤ 一次　8月第4日曜日
　　　└ 二次　9月第4日曜日
　　　　　　　※実践レベルのみ

📖 検定時間 🏷

一次試験

基礎（65分）9時30分～

標準（70分）11時30分～

実践（80分）13時30分～

📖 検定方法 🏷

各地一般会場

オンライン（個人・団体）

団体指定会場

📖 検定料金 🏷

※団体受検は検定料から1,000引き

基礎　　¥5,000

標準　　¥7,000

実践　　¥9,000

📖 検定内容 🏷

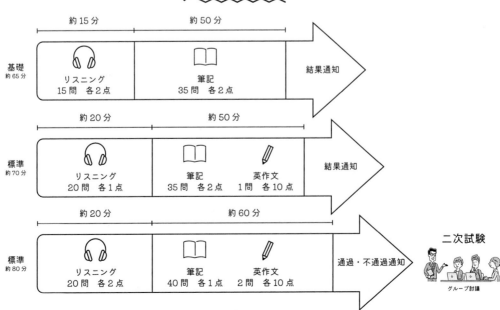

	約15分	約50分	
基礎 約65分	🎧 リスニング 15問 各2点	📖 筆記 35問 各2点	結果通知

	約20分	約50分	
標準 約70分	🎧 リスニング 20問 各1点	📖 筆記 35問 各2点 / ✏️ 英作文 1問 各10点	結果通知

	約20分	約60分	
標準 約80分	🎧 リスニング 20問 各2点	📖 筆記 40問 各1点 / ✏️ 英作文 2問 各10点	通過・不通過通知

二次試験

グループ討議

教職英語検定実施要領

申込方法

個人受検

STEP 1 ホームページを確認

STEP 2 受検方法、会場を選択して申込

STEP 3 お支払を各方法で完了する
- カード払い
- 銀行振込
- 郵便局振替
- コンビニ払い
- その他マルチ決済

STEP 4 受検のご案内がメールに届く

STEP 5 各会場またはオンラインで受検

団体受検

STEP 1 事務局へご連絡ください

STEP 2 団体番号を発行

STEP 3 団体責任者の団体申込をする

STEP 4 検定料のお支払
方法1）各受検者が個人受検者と同じ方法で申込・お支払をする
方法1）団体責任者が全受検者のお支払をまとめて当協会指定口座へ振込をする

STEP 5 団体会場またはオンラインでの実施

資格証

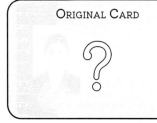

ORIGINAL CARD

?

教職英語検定合格者へ

特別な資格証を発行しています。

申込・詳細はホームページにてご確認ください。

※記載内容は改訂されることがあります。最新情報はホームページを確認下さい。

www.senseieigo.com

教職英語検定小学校担当用テキスト　第2巻

2023年11月1日初版1刷発行

著　者　　一般社団法人 教職英語検定協会
〒224-0003　東京都目黒区中目黒 3-6-2　F・S ビル 5 階
TEL　　03-5725-0553
Fax　　03-6452-4148
Web　https://www.senseieigo.com

発売所　　株式会社　ブックフォレ
〒113-0033　神奈川県横浜市都筑区中川中央 1-20-15-201
TEL　　03-5800-8494
Fax　　03-5800-5353
Web　　https://bookfore.co.jp/

印刷・製本　冊子印刷社

テキストブック読み上げ音源ダウンロードリンク

https://bookfore.co.jp/glh/download/

本書掲載写真・イラストについて
1. イラストライター 千野六久 様 (http://rokuhisachino.tumblr.com)
2. かわいいフリー素材集 いらすとや みふね たかし 様 (https://www.irasutoya.com)
等のイラストを掲載しております。
本書掲載させて頂いたイラスト・写真については、使用のご快諾とご協力を頂いております。
上記の方々のホームページには、大変素晴らしいイラストデザイン集が掲載されています。
生徒への指導に当たってのご参考、また、より分かりやすい教材、プリント作成等に
活用できるものが多数ですので、是非、多くの先生方にご覧頂きたい次第です。
多くの方々の著作物を掲載させて頂き、より分かりやすい教材となりました。お礼申し上げます。